Read-Aloud Story

and

Activity Book

Vol. 1

Gospel Light

How to Make Clean Copies from This Book

YOU MAY MAKE COPIES OF PORTIONS OF THIS BOOK WITH A CLEAN CONSCIENCE IF

- you (or someone in your organization) are the original purchaser;
- you are using the copies you make for a noncommercial purpose (such as teaching or promoting your ministry) within your church or organization;
- you follow the instructions provided in this book.

HOWEVER, IT IS ILLEGAL FOR YOU TO MAKE COPIES IF

- you are using the material to promote, advertise or sell a product or service other than for ministry fund-raising;
- you are using the material in or on a product for sale; or
- you or your organization are not the original purchaser of this book.

By following these guidelines you help us keep our products affordable.

Thank you,
Gospel Light

Editorial Staff

Publisher, William T. Greig

Senior Consulting Publisher, Dr. Elmer L. Towns

Publisher, Research, Planning and Development, Billie Baptiste

Managing Editor, Lynnette Pennings, M.A.

Senior Consulting Editor, Wesley Haystead, M.S.Ed.

Senior Editor, Biblical and Theological Issues, Bayard Taylor, M.Div.

Senior Advisor, Biblical and Theological Issues, Dr. Gary S. Greig

Senior Editor, Sheryl Haystead

Editorial Team, Mary Gross, Jay Bea Summerfield

Contributing Editor, Linda Mattia

Designer, Zelle Olson

Contents

How to Use This Book

IF YOU TEACH ALONE:

1. Prepare pages from the *Read-Aloud Story and Activity Book, Vol. I* by making a double-sided photocopy for each child in your class. Provide crayons or markers for children to use in coloring the pages. Plan ahead for those pages that require a few extra materials (tape, construction paper, etc.).

2. The pages may be used at a variety of times—for early arrivals, for children who finish other activities ahead of time or for children who need a quiet change of pace. You may also occasionally substitute the sheets for another activity suggested in your curriculum, or offer them in addition to the suggested activities. Have extra photocopies on hand during holiday times, so there are enough for visitors.

3. Read the story and use the Let's Talk About the Story ideas as children color. If you are unable to read the story aloud and ask the questions, label each page with the child's name to send home. Encourage parents to read and discuss the story at home.

IF YOU TEACH WITH ONE OR MORE OTHER TEACHERS:

Plan a time in your session schedule when pages from the *Read-Aloud Story and Activity Book, Vol. I* may be used (see number 2 above). Assign one teacher to prepare and lead the activity. He or she may read the story on the sheet as children color. Help children apply Bible truth to their lives by using the Let's Talk About Story ideas on the back of each sheet.

IF YOU ARE THE DIRECTOR OR COORDINATOR:

Use pages from the *Read-Aloud Story and Activity Book, Vol. I* to supplement your regular children's programs.

1. Distribute sheets for children to complete during transition times between childrens' programs.
2. Attach each page to a clipboard. Distribute clipboards and small boxes of crayons to children who come to an adult service.
3. Use the pages during meeting times when child care is not available or when teachers are unexpectedly absent.
4. At a family camp or event, lead families to complete one or more pages as part of the event activities.
5. Use the pages as part of Sunday evening or weekday early childhood programs.
6. When children are participating in choir performances or other special programs, provide pages and crayons for waiting children.

"God cares about you." (See 1 Peter 5:7.)

Cut and fold on lines indicated to make pages. After folding, pages should be in order from 1 to 4.
Tape them to activity page. Color the picture.

Tape pages here.

Cut.

| 4 | | FOLD 2 | 1 | 2 | FOLD 1 | Cut. | 3 |

FOLD 1

FOLD 2

Cut.

Read-Aloud Story and Activity

1. Make a copy of Story Picture 1 for yourself and each child. Gather materials; color and complete your copy.
2. **Listen to find out what this family is doing.** Read story and show completed Story Picture 1.
3. Distribute materials. Use Let's Talk About the Story ideas as children complete pictures.

Mom's Big Book

Mom was working on her big book. She was cutting paper with her fancy scissors. Katlyn and Blake were helping Mom. They were cutting paper with their scissors, too.

Mom's special book lay open on the table. It was full of pictures!

Katlyn asked, "Mom, can we read a story?"

Mom laughed. "I was just about to tell you a story," she said. Mom opened her book to the very front.

Blake said, "That isn't a story book, Mom."

Mom said, "Oh, yes it is! It is a book all about your story and Katlyn's story. Look at this page!"

Blake and Katlyn looked. There was a picture of twin babies. They were little and red and wrinkled. "Who is THAT?" asked Katlyn.

"Those babies are you and Blake. Once, you were both very little! You looked pretty funny, didn't you? But you didn't stay little.

"I sure didn't!" said Blake. "I'm not a baby. I'm BIG now!"

"That's right," said Mom. "You grew and grew just as God planned for you to do. And God gave you to Daddy and me so we could take care of you."

Mom turned the page. The babies in the next pictures weren't so little. They weren't red and wrinkly. These babies were crawling and playing!

Mom pointed to another picture. "Before long," she said, "those babies had learned to walk all by themselves! And look! There is a picture of two birthday cakes!"

"The cakes each have two candles on them!" said Katlyn. "I remember that doll in the picture. I still have that doll!" She ran to get her doll.

Blake looked up at his mom. "I'm glad God gave me a family. I like you and Daddy and Katlyn."

Mom gave Blake a big hug. "I'm glad too. That's one way God shows He cares about us, by giving us each other!"

Let's Talk About the Story

What kind of book did Mom read to Blake and Katlyn? Do you have a book at home like that? What special story was in the book? Who made Blake and Katlyn's family?

Who are the people God made for your family? God gave each of us a family to love and help us. Our Bible says, "God cares about you." **Let's say this Bible verse together.** Repeat Bible verse with children. **We can thank God for our families.** Pray briefly.

"God said, 'I am with you and will watch over you wherever you go.'" (See Genesis 28:15.)

Color the picture. Draw a gift inside the box. Cut wrapping paper and tape it to the box. Tape a piece of ribbon on box lid.

(Tape paper at top only.)

Read-Aloud Story and Activity

1. Make a copy of Story Picture 2 for yourself and each child. Gather materials; color and complete your copy.
2. **Listen for ways Casey's family helped him.** Read story and show completed Story Picture 2.
3. Distribute materials. Use Let's Talk About the Story ideas as children complete pictures.

Who Helped Casey?

Casey was in his bedroom. He was excited! He pulled his new shirt over his head. He looked under the bed for his shoes. He was getting ready for his friend Kevin's birthday party. He ran to find his mom.

"I like birthday parties!" Casey said as he ran into the bathroom. "We're going to play games and eat cake and ice cream."

"Parties are lots of fun," Mom laughed as she swung Casey onto the counter. "So are you. Sit very still now, so I can get your hair brushed."

It was hard for Casey to sit still when he was so excited! But he did it. "There," said Mom. "Daddy said he would clean up your shoes. Run to the kitchen to see if he's finished." Casey hurried to the kitchen.

Dad smiled at Casey. "Here are your shoes, son!" Daddy said. "I think you're just about ready for the party." Casey put on his shoes and Daddy tied them. "Now you're ready. Let's get in the car!"

Suddenly Casey stopped. He got a worried look on his face. "Where's my present for Kevin?" Casey asked.

"I just finished wrapping it," Mom said. She handed it to Casey.

In the car, Daddy and Casey talked. Dad asked, "How many places have we gone today already?"

Casey thought a minute. "Well, we went to the store to get Kevin's present. We went to another store to buy my new shirt. We went to the park where I got my shoes in the mud puddle. Then we went home."

"Who was with you in all those places?" Daddy asked

"You were! You took me to the store and the park. I saw Ryan at the park. He was with me for a while, playing. Mom was with me at home, too." Casey said.

"Do you know who else was with you in all those places?" Daddy asked. "God was with you! God says He is with us wherever we go!" Daddy stopped the car in front of Kevin's house. As Casey got out, he gave Daddy a big hug. "Now God will be with me at Kevin's party, too!" he said.

Let's Talk About the Story

Why was Casey excited? Why did he like birthday parties? What do you think Casey gave Kevin for his birthday? What are some of the places Casey went? Who was with him?

Our Bible says, "God said, "I am with you and will watch over you wherever you go.' " Let's say this Bible verse together. Repeat Bible verse with children. **Let's pray. We can thank God that He is always with us.** Pray briefly.

"I thank and praise you, O God." Daniel 2:23

Connect the dots. Color the picture. Draw and color what Nina found under the pillow. Glue a piece of red yarn on the cap.

Story Picture 3

Read-Aloud Story and Activity

1. Make a copy of Story Picture 3 for yourself and each child. Gather materials; color and complete your copy.

2. **Listen to find out what this girl is looking for.** Read story and show completed Story Picture 3.

3. Distribute materials. Use Let's Talk About the Story ideas as children complete pictures.

Nina's Suprise

It was a cold, snowy afternoon. Nina was taking her nap. Grandma peeked into Nina's room and whispered to herself, "I think I can finish knitting Nina's cap before she gets up from her nap, but I'll have to hurry!"

Grandma went to her room and quickly took out the red yarn and the knitting needles from her closet. The cap was a surprise for Nina! Grandma smiled as she thought about how Nina might like her new cap.

Soon Grandma was knitting. Clickety, clickety, clickety—the needles made a happy sound as she worked. The sun was beginning to shine and the snow clouds were leaving.

Nina woke up. The sun was coming through her window. She smiled and jumped up. Now she could make a snowman with Grandma! Then Nina stopped. She could hear a very strange sound. Clickety, clickety, clickety. Was it the old clock in the living room? She ran to the living room. It wasn't the clock. Was it the sewing machine? Nina ran to the sewing machine. No one was there. What WAS that sound? She tiptoed down the hall and stopped at Grandma's door. The sound was coming from Grandma's room!

Nina knocked on the door. "Grandma," she said. "What are you doing?"

Nina opened the door. Grandma was smiling. She had knitting needles in her hand.

"What are you knitting? I don't see any yarn!" Nina said as she came closer.

Grandma said, "Look under my pillow and you'll get a surprise!"

Nina looked at Grandma's bed. There was a tiny bit of something red sticking out. She reached under the pillow and pulled out a bright red cap! Nina pulled the cap down over her head. It felt snug and soft and warm!

Grandma held up a mirror. "Look! I wanted to surprise you before we went out to make our snowman!"

Nina hugged Grandma. "Oh, Grandma! Thank you! I love my new cap! Now my ears will stay warm!"

And then Nina and Grandma went outside and built the biggest snowman they could build!

Let's Talk About the Story

Why did Grandma do her knitting while Nina was asleep? What did Nina think might be making the sounds of the knitting needles? What did Nina say after she found the cap?

What are some ways the people at your house show they love you? God gives us people to love us and care for us. God always cares for us. God's Word says, "I thank and praise you, O God." Repeat Bible verse with children. **Let's think of some reasons to thank God. We can thank God anytime.** Pray briefly.

"Lord, you are good to us." (See Psalm 86:5.)

Connect the dots. Glue grass or hay in cow's manger.
Draw more corn in pig's trough. Color the picture.

Story Picture 4

Read-Aloud Story and Activity

1. Make a copy of Story Picture 4 for yourself and each child. Gather materials; color and complete your copy.

2. **Listen for the kinds of animals this boy met.** Read story and show completed Story Picture 4.

3. Distribute materials. Use Let's Talk About the Story ideas as children complete pictures.

On the Farm

Nathan woke up. The sun was coming up. He jumped out of bed. It was time for what Nathan liked best! He was visiting his uncle's farm. And early morning was time to feed the animals and milk the cows!

Nathan dressed and ran downstairs. He followed Uncle Steve into the barn and then helped him throw hay to the cows. Nathan watched the cows munch the hay. "Do the cows ever say 'Thank you' for their hay?" Nathan asked.

Uncle Steve laughed. "No, I guess they're too busy eating!" he said.

"Now it's the kittens' turn to eat," Uncle Steve said. He poured milk into the kittens' pan.

"Here, kitty, kitty, kitty," Nathan called. "Here's your breakfast." The kittens came running. They crowded around the pan and lapped up the milk. Soon it was all gone. "Mew mew! Mew mew!" they said.

"I think they're saying 'More milk!'" Uncle Steve laughed.

Nathan and Uncle Steve went to the pigpen. "We'll throw some corn to the pigs," Uncle Steve said. The pigs gobbled up the corn! Their noisy oink-oink-oink didn't sound a bit like "Thank you."

"Now let's feed the chickens and ducks," Uncle Steve said. He and Nathan threw handfuls of grain onto the ground. Those chickens and ducks made a lot of noise! They clucked and quacked. But Nathan noticed they never said "Thank you" either.

When they were finished with their chores, Nathan and Uncle Steve came in to have their own breakfast. Uncle Steve thanked God for their food. "God, thank You for our food," Uncle Steve said.

"All the animals on this farm eat and eat and EAT," said Nathan, "but they never say 'Thank you.'"

"Well, we people are the ones who should be thankful," said Uncle Steve. "God gives us the animals. They give food to us. What food does the cow give?"

"Milk," Nathan answered, setting down his milk glass. "And then people make ice cream and cheese and butter."

"What do the chickens give us?" asked Uncle Steve.

"They lay the eggs!" Nathan said. "I found two eggs just this morning!"

"God planned for us to have the food we need," Uncle Steve said. "And God's plan is good."

Let's Talk About the Story

Where was Nathan visiting? What animals lived on Uncle Steve's farm? What animals ate hay? Corn? Grain? Drank milk? What did Uncle Steve do before he ate breakfast? What food do cows give us? Chickens?

God shows His love for us by giving us food and water. Our Bible says, "Lord, you are good to us." Repeat Bible verse with children. **Let's thank God for food and water.** Pray briefly.

"I love the Lord." Psalm 116:1

Color the picture. Glue pieces of string for the swing ropes.

Story Picture 5

Read-Aloud Story and Activity

1. Make a copy of Story Picture 5 for yourself and each child. Gather materials; color and complete your copy.

2. **Listen to find out what this girl prayed**. Read story and show completed Story Picture 5.

3. Distribute materials. Use Let's Talk About the Story ideas as children complete pictures.

The Promise

"Daddy," called Leah as she ran into the living room. "Will you make me a swing?"

"Where would we hang a swing?" he asked.

"We could hang it in the basement or out in the barn," Leah answered.

"Let's go out to the barn and see if we can find a place to hang a swing."

Daddy and Leah put on their coats and went out to the barn. Daddy looked carefully at the rafters. "I think that board is strong enough to hold a swing," he said. "I promise to make you a swing, but I can't do it today. You will have to wait until I have time."

Leah jumped up and down. "Thank you. Thank you, Daddy!" she said.

The next day Leah was playing outside. *Maybe Daddy will make my swing today,* she thought. She prayed, "Dear God, please help Daddy make my swing!"

But Daddy didn't make the swing that day. One, two, three, four days passed; and still Daddy didn't have time to make the swing. Every night when Leah went to bed, she prayed, "Dear God, please help Daddy make my swing." Daddy had promised. She was sure it would happen. But it was hard to wait!

The next afternoon Leah was playing with the kittens in the barn. Daddy came in carrying his tall ladder, a board with holes in it and a strong rope.

"Today I have time to make the swing I promised you," he said to Leah. "Come on. You can help me."

Leah helped Daddy carry the rope over to the center of the barn. First, Daddy put the rope through the holes in the seat. He tied big knots in each end. Then he carried the rope up, up the ladder. Daddy tied each end of the rope to the strong rafter. He made sure the rope was tight, so it wouldn't slip.

"Now let's see how your swing works," he said. First, Daddy sat down on the swing to be sure it was very strong. Then he picked up Leah and set her down in the swing. Daddy gave her a push. Up, up, up she went. Down, down, down she came. Up and down. Up and down. It was fun!

"Wheee! This is a good swing," Leah said. "Thank you, Daddy. You promised, I prayed, and the swing got made!"

Let's Talk About the Story

What did Leah ask Daddy? What did Daddy promise Leah? What did Leah pray about? Where did Daddy put the swing?

Our Bible says, "I love the Lord." "Lord" is another name for God. Because we love God, we can talk to Him anytime. Because He loves us, He is always glad to hear us and help us! Let's tell God how much we love Him. Pray briefly with children.

"Whatever you do, do your work for the Lord." (See Colossians 3:23.)

Color the picture. Draw a line to help Dane find trash to pick up.

Read-Aloud Story and Activity

1. Make a copy of Story Picture 6 for yourself and each child. Gather matrials; color and complete your copy.

2. **Listen for ways this family helped at church.** Read story and show completed Story Picture 6.

3. Distribute materials. Use Let's Talk About the Story ideas as children complete pictures.

Helping at Church

"Dane," Mother called, "grab your jacket. It's time to go to church."

That's funny, Dane thought. *This isn't Sunday. It's not the day we go to church.* Then he remembered. Today was work day at the church building. And Mother had said he and Mariah were old enough to help!

After breakfast, Mother, Mariah and Dane hurried out of the house. As Dane ran down the steps, he tripped. When he fell, he cut his hand. "OUCH!"

Mother looked at the cut. "It will be all right," she said. "I'll clean it and put a bandage on it. Your hand will feel better." While Mother bandaged his hand, Dane cried big tears. "Now I can't go to work at the church building," he sobbed.

"Maybe we can find things for you to do with one hand!" Mother said. She gave Dane a hug, and soon they were on their way to the church.

When Mother, Mariah and Dane got to church, lots of people were already there. "Dane and Mariah, you can help me clean the two- and three-year-olds' room," said Mom. Together they walked to the room. "You may take the toys off the shelves, and I'll wash them," Mom told Mariah.

"Dane, these puzzle pieces are all mixed up. Do you think you can separate the pieces and put the puzzles together?" Mom asked.

"These puzzles are easy," Dane answered. "I can work them with one hand." He began putting puzzles together while Mom and Mariah cleaned the toys.

Dane soon finished putting all the puzzles together. "What else can I do to help?" he asked.

"This box of crayons needs sorting. Please take out all the broken pieces," Mom said. Dane began sorting the crayons. "This is easy to do with one hand," he said. When he finished with the crayons, he asked, "Can I do work outside?"

"Well, let's see," Mom said. "What kind of job can you do with one hand?" She thought for a minute. Then she said, "I know! You can pick up trash that has blown into the church yard."

So Dane walked all around the yard picking up every scrap he could find.

Soon it was time to go home. Dane, Mariah and Mom said good-bye to their friends. "It was fun helping at the church building," Mariah said. "I helped, too," Dane said, holding up his bandaged hand. "I helped with just one hand!"

Let's Talk About the Story

What happened to Dane at his house? How did Dane's mother help him? How did Dane help at the church building? How did Mariah help at the church building? What are some ways you can help at our church?

Because we love God, we do our best work. It's another way to show God we love Him. Our Bible says, "Whatever you do, do your work for the Lord." Repeat Bible verse with children. **We can also pray and tell God we love Him.** Pray briefly with children.

"Come and listen to the words of the Lord." (See Joshua 3:9.)

Color the first picture in each row. Color the picture that matches the first picture in each row.

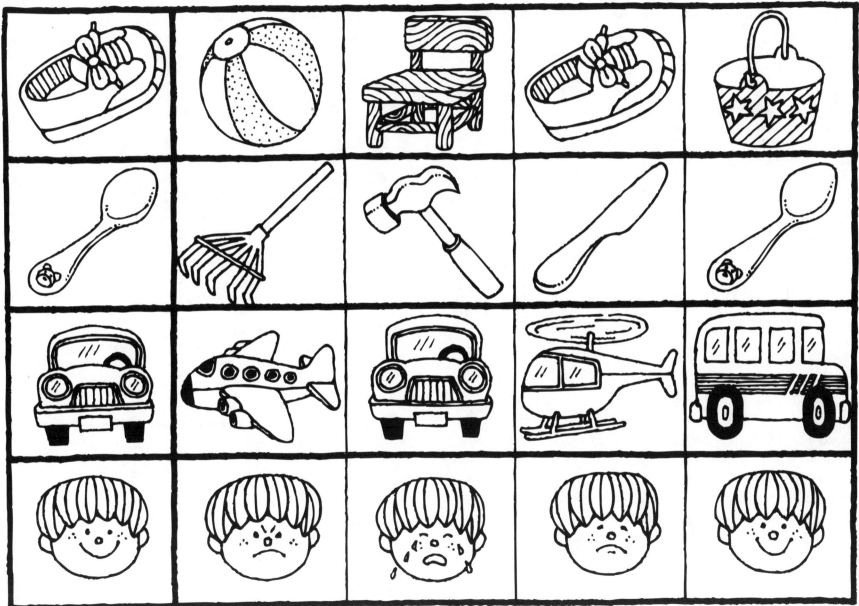

Story Picture 7

Read-Aloud Story and Activity

1. Make a copy of Story Picture 7 for yourself and each child. Gather materials; color and complete your copy.
2. **Listen to find out what this boy was missing.** Read story and show completed Story Picture 7.
3. Distribute materials. Use Let's Talk About the Story ideas as children complete pictures.

Where's My Shoe?

"Get up, Channing!" Dad called. "Today is the day we go to church."

Quickly Channing jumped out of bed. Church day! He was glad. He liked to go to church. Channing took off his pajamas and put on the clothes his dad had laid out for him. He was all dressed, except for one shoe.

Where is my other shoe? Channing wondered. He called, "Dad, where is my shoe?" as he dived under the bed. He couldn't hear what Dad said.

Channing came out from under the bed. He had found his blue car and three gum wrappers but no shoe. How could he go with only ONE SHOE?

"Dad!" Channing called. "I can't find my SHOE!" Then he went into the closet. He couldn't hear what his dad said back to him.

Channing couldn't find his shoe in the closet either. He found a seashell and some string he forgot he had, but his shoe was GONE!

Once more Channing called out, "DAD! PLEASE help me find my shoe!" THEN Channing stood still and listened. He heard his dad's voice.

Dad said, "Channing, can you hear me? I TOLD you where your shoe is!" Dad came into the room and held up Channing's shoe.

"Your shoe was in my hand the whole time! It needed a new shoelace," Dad said. "You would have known where it was if you'd stopped to listen!"

Channing laughed. "Thank you, Daddy. Now will you please help me tie my shoes?" he asked. Dad and Channing worked at tying the shoes and soon they were on their way to the kitchen for breakfast. They ate and then went to church. Channing went to his class.

"Good morning, Channing," his teacher said. "I'm glad you came to church! Today we're going to listen to God's Word."

Channing smiled a big smile. He said, "I KNOW about listening. I listened already today! And when I did, I found my shoe!"

Let's Talk About the Story

What did Channing do after he asked his dad where his shoe was the first time? The second time? Where was his other shoe? What are some times it is hard to listen?

Our Bible says, "Come and listen to the words of the Lord." Repeat Bible verse with children. **One way we show we love God is by listening to His Word. Let's thank God for the people who tell us His Word.** Pray briefly.

"We must obey God." Acts 5:29
Color the picture.
Draw a line to show the ways Michael helped.

START

END

Story Picture 8

Read-Aloud Story and Activity

1. Make a copy of Story Picture 8 for yourself and each child. Gather materials; color and complete your copy.

2. **Listen to hear how this boy felt.** Read story and show completed Story Picture 8.

3. Distribute materials. Use Let's Talk About the Story ideas as children complete pictures.

Who Was the Helper?

"Michael," Mom called. "I want you to come with me to the store."

"I don't want to go. I want to stay here and play," Michael said.

"I'm sorry, Michael; but since Dad and Mark are at the soccer game, I can't leave you here alone," Mom said. Michael started to feel angry. He really did want to stay home and play! Then Michael remembered. Doing what Mom said showed love for God and his mom, too. So he took a deep breath. He picked up a toy to play with in the car and went along without grumbling.

At the store Mom bought lots of food. Michael saw some of his favorite foods: apples, carrots, milk and chicken. When they arrived home, Michael said, "I'm hungry. I want something to eat."

"You'll have to wait until I put away all these bags of food." Michael started to feel angry. He wanted to eat RIGHT NOW. Then he remembered that doing what Mom said was a way to show he loved God. So he took a deep breath. He went outside to wait until lunch was ready.

After lunch, Michael played with his cars until Mom said, "Nap time!" This time, Michael started to feel REALLY angry. He didn't want to stop playing with his cars! Then he remembered that obeying was a good way to show his love. So he took a deep breath. He put down his cars and found his teddy bear.

That night as Mom helped Michael get ready for bed, she said, "I know a boy that was a good helper today. He came along to the store without fussing. He waited for his lunch. He took his nap. Do you know who that good helper is?"

Michael laughed. "I guess it's me!"

Let's Talk About the Story

Where did Mom and Michael go? Why didn't he want to go? How did he feel? Why couldn't Mom fix his lunch when he wanted it? How did he feel? Why didn't Michael want to take a nap? What did Michael remember?

When are some times it can be hard to obey? Our Bible says, "We must obey God." Let's say this Bible verse together. Repeat Bible verse with children. **We can ask God to help us show we love Him by obeying Him.** Pray briefly.

✗

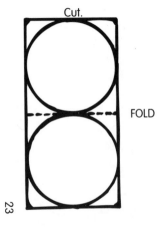

Cut.

FOLD

23

"With love, help each other." (See Galatians 5:13.)

Cut and fold ball on lines as indicated. Tape sides together.
Tape string to ball and to ✗ so ball swings freely. Color the picture.

Read-Aloud Story and Activity

1. Make a copy of Story Picture 9 for yourself and each child. Gather materials; color and complete your copy.
2. **Listen to find out what these children are doing**. Read story and show completed Story Picture 9.
3. Distribute materials. Use Let's Talk About the Story ideas as children complete pictures.

Jonathan's Visit

"Alex! Cassie!" Mom called from the back door. "Please come here. It's time to put on clean clothes. Mrs. Hill and little Jonathan will soon be here to visit us," Mom said.

"Jonathan is too little to play with," Cassie grumbled.

"He can't even reach the pedals on my tricycle," Alex said.

"He puts my doll's hair in his mouth!" Cassie said.

"Jonathan isn't old enough to do all the things you can do. But we want Jonathan to have a happy time when he visits us. So let's think of things he CAN do," Mom suggested.

Alex and Cassie were quiet. They were thinking as Mom helped them put on their clean clothes.

Slowly Alex said, "Well, we can roll the ball to Jonathan, and he can roll it back."

"Jonathan can sit in the wagon and we can pull him." Cassie suggested.

"And he laughs when we stack up blocks for him," Alex added.

"He can ride our rocking horse," Cassie said.

"Those are good things to play with Jonathan," Mom said. "I know you will help him have a happy time."

Bing-bong! Bing-bong! It was the doorbell. Cassie went with Mom to open the door. There stood Mrs. Hill and little Jonathan. Cassie took Jonathan to the playroom. While Mom talked with Mrs. Hill, Alex and Cassie played with Jonathan.

"Let's play with the ball, Jonathan," Alex said.

Jonathan was too little to talk much. But he could hold out his hands and smile. Alex and Cassie took turns rolling the ball to Jonathan. They rolled the ball to him and he rolled it back to them. Alex and Cassie laughed and laughed as they tried to reach the ball. It rolled every which way. Jonathan was too little to roll the ball straight.

Soon Jonathan was tired of playing ball. So Alex and Cassie stacked up the blocks for him. Ka-plunk! Jonathan squealed with laughter as he made the blocks tumble down. Alex and Cassie piled up the blocks again and again. And Jonathan laughed as he made them tumble down.

"I like to play with Jonathan," Alex said as he helped to rock Jonathan on the rocking horse.

"Me, too!" Cassie said happily.

Before Mrs. Hill took little Jonathan home, she said to Alex and Cassie, "Thank you for helping Jonathan have good time!"

"You helped me, too!" Mom said. "You helped me have a good visit with Mrs. Hill while you had a good time with little Jonathan!"

Let's Talk About the Story

Why didn't Alex and Cassie want to play with Jonathan? What did Alex and Cassie do to help little Jonathan have good time? How did Alex and Cassie help Mom have a good visit with Mrs. Hill?

One way to show God's love is by helping other people. Our Bible says, "With love, help each other." Let's say this Bible verse together. Repeat Bible verse with children. **We can ask God to help us love people and show we love them by helping them.** Pray briefly.

"Do not forget to do good."
Hebrews 13:16

Name the things the Miller family used to get ready for school and work. Name the people in their family. Color the picture in the first box in Row 1. Color the matching picture in Row 1. Do the same in each row.

Read-Aloud Story and Activity

1. Make a copy of Story Picture 10 for yourself and each child. Color and complete your copy.

2. **Listen for ways this family helped each other.** Read story and show completed Story Picture 10.

3. Distribute materials. Use Let's Talk About the Story ideas as children complete pictures.

A Family of Helpers

"Michelle, PLEASE hold still while I brush your hair!" Mom said.

"But Anna hasn't tied my shoes yet!" Michelle answered.

"I know," her mother said. "Sometimes it is hard to wait. But it helps if you don't wiggle. We have lots to do this morning. We have to work together."

This morning it was hard to remember to help each other get ready for school and work. It was hard for Michelle to hold still while Mom brushed her hair. It was hard for Mom and Dad to fix breakfast and pack lunches. It was hard for Anna to remember to tie her sister's shoes. Everyone came to the breakfast table feeling a little cranky.

When everyone sat down to eat breakfast, Dad prayed, "Dear God, sometimes it's hard for us to be helpful to each other. Show us ways today that we can be kind to each other. In Jesus' name, amen."

Everyone stopped for a minute. Mom said, "Anna, I will try to help you finish your school project tonight."

Anna said, "Michelle, I will try to tie your shoes tomorrow as soon as you get them on."

Michelle said to Mom, "Mommy, I will try to hold still tomorrow while you brush my hair."

Daddy smiled at everyone. He said, "And I will pack the lunches and try to smile! That's a way we can all help each other!"

Soon it was time for everyone to leave. Michelle's hair was brushed and her shoes were tied. Anna was ready. Mom was ready. Dad was ready.

"Let's go, Mom," shouted Anna as she started down the hall. "Beat you to the elevator, Daddy!" called Michelle. The family was off and running!

Let's Talk About the Story

Where were the people in this family getting ready to go? What was hard for Michelle to do? For Anna? For Mom and Dad? What did Dad do before the family ate? When is it hard for you to hold still? To wait?

Who are the people God made for your family? Sometimes it's hard to help each other in our families. Our Bible says, "Do not forget to do good." Let's say this Bible verse together. Repeat Bible verse with children. **We can ask God to help us show love in our families.** Pray briefly.

"We love because he first loved us." 1 John 4:19

Draw in the missing lines. Color the picture. Put an ✗ on the places Andrew looked.

Story Picture 24

Read-Aloud Story and Activity

1. Make a copy of Story Picture 24 for yourself and each child. Gather materials; color and complete your copy.

2. **Listen to find out what this boy is doing.** Read story and show completed Story Picture 24.

3. Distribute materials. Use Let's Talk About the Story ideas as children complete pictures.

The Lost Kitten

Andrew was in the sandbox, building roads and racing his cars. He moved the blue car over a hill. He zoomed a red around a curve. Suddenly Andrew heard a strange sound. It sounded squeaky. It sounded sad. Andrew looked around. Where was that sound coming from?

Then Andrew heard the sound again. Maybe it was a kitten! Andrew got out of the sandbox to look around. He heard the sound again. Yes. It sounded like a kitten, all right! Andrew looked all around the house. He looked under the car and behind the bushes. But he couldn't see any kitten ANYWHERE!

Andrew heard the little sound again. It was coming from up high! Andrew ran to the tree. He looked up. He moved his head this way and that way. Finally he saw it. A black and white kitten was holding on to a branch way up in the tree. The kitten saw Andrew. It mewed loudly. It looked like it was afraid.

Andrew knew just what to do. He said to the kitten, "It's OK. I'll help you!" He ran into the house where his daddy was working.

"Daddy! Daddy!" he said, all out of breath. "There's a kitten in the tree outside my window. It's way high up in the tree and it can't get down!"

Daddy thought a minute. Then he said, "I'm glad you want to help the kitten! It's near your window, you say? Let's go upstairs and look from up high."

That was a good idea! Andrew and his dad raced upstairs. Daddy opened Andrew's bedroom window. He removed the window screen and set it in Andrew's room. Then he leaned part way out the window. Andrew stood by the window and held his breath! Daddy looked around carefully and then reached out his hand. The kitten was so close to Andrew's window, it was easy for Daddy to reach it!

When Daddy brought the kitten in, Andrew could see that it was Heather's kitten. He said, "Daddy, I bet Heather is worried about her kitten. I'll take it across the street to her house."

"OK," Daddy said. "I'll go with you."

They brought the kitten to Heather's house and rang the bell. Heather's mom came to the door. She was VERY glad to see the kitten! "We've been looking all over for her. Thank you for helping!"

Andrew decided to stay and play with Heather and her kitten. He liked that kitten. He was glad he could be kind to the kitten and to Heather, too!

Let's Talk About the Story

What noise did Andrew hear? Where did he look for the kitten? Where was the kitten? How did Daddy get the kitten out of the tree? How did Heather feel when she saw the kitten?

Because God loves us, we can show love to others, too. Our Bible says, "We love, because he first loved us." Let's say this Bible verse together. Repeat Bible verse with children. **Let's thank God for loving us. And let's ask Him to help us show His love to others!** Pray briefly.

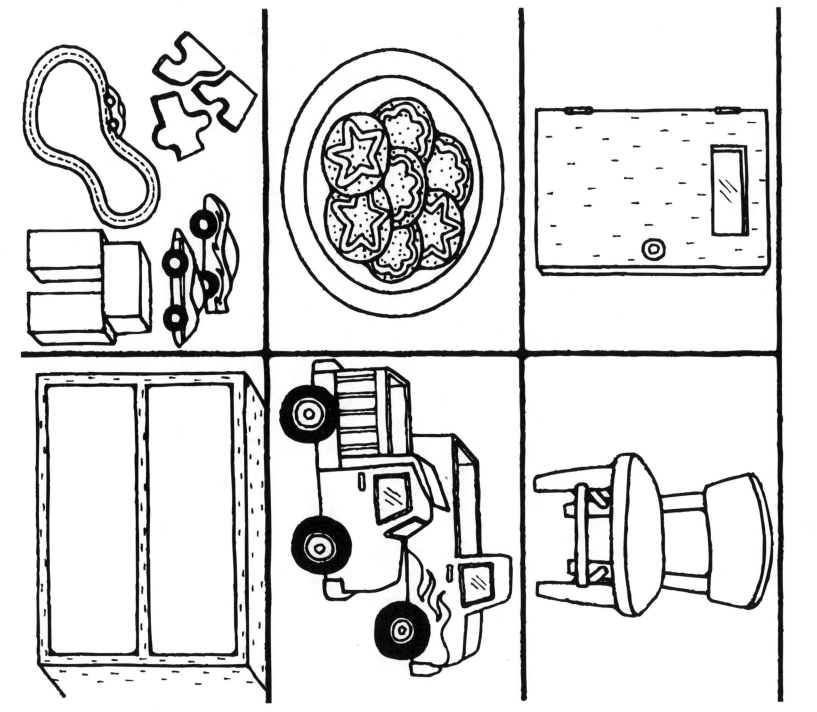

"A friend loves at all times." Proverbs 17:17

Each picture shows something Max or Jeff used to show kindness.
In the last box, draw what you think Jeff did with the toys before he went home. Color the pictures.

Story Picture 11

Read-Aloud Story and Activity

1. Make a copy of Story Picture 11 for yourself and each child. Gather materials; color and complete your copy.

2. **Listen to find out what this boy did to be kind.** Read story and show completed Story Picture 11.

3. Distribute materials. Use Let's Talk About the Story ideas as children complete pictures.

Max's Visitors

Bing-bong! Bing-bong! The doorbell at Max's house was ringing. Max's mother was busy, so Max ran to open the door. There stood his friend Jeff and Jeff's mother.

"Come in," Max said. He opened the door wide and smiled a big smile! While Max's mother and Jeff's mother talked, Max showed Jeff to his room. He held up his two best trucks. "Which truck do you want to play with?" Max asked. Jeff chose the red one. Max and Jeff played with the trucks.

"Let's build a ramp for these trucks," Jeff said. Max and Jeff built a ramp out of blocks and some wood. They rolled their trucks up the ramp. Then they let them go to see how far the trucks would roll. It was fun!

Then Mother called, "Time for juice and cookies!"

Max and Jeff came running to the kitchen. "Those cookies look good!" Max said. But even though he wanted a cookie RIGHT NOW, Max passed the plate of cookies to Jeff first. Jeff chose a cookie with pink frosting. Max chose a cookie with green frosting. They each got a glass of juice and ate their cookies.

After the boys finished eating, they went back to Max's room. They played with the ramp and Max's cars. They put the cars on Max's racetrack. They built a town with blocks. Then they worked some puzzles.

Soon Jeff's mother called, "Jeff, it's time to go home." Jeff looked around. Puzzles, blocks, cars and pieces of the racing track were scattered all over! When Jeff looked at Max's toy shelf, he had an idea. Before he went home, what do you think Jeff did?

Let's Talk About the Story

What did Max do when he heard the doorbell? Which truck did Jeff choose to play with? What did Max do before he took a cookie? What other toys did the boys play with? How do you think Jeff showed he was a kind friend before he went home?

What are some ways you show your friends you are glad for them? When we are kind, it shows God's love. Our Bible says, "A friend loves at all times." Let's say this Bible verse together. Repeat Bible verse with children. **Let's thank God for our friends. Let's ask God to help us be kind to them.** Pray briefly.

"Do good to all people." Galatians 6:10

Draw blocks to make Joshua's racetrack. Color the picture.

Read-Aloud Story and Activity

1. Make a copy of Story Picture 12 for yourself and each child. Gather materials; color and complete your copy.

2. **Listen for ways this boy was kind to this girl.** Read story and show completed Story Picture 12.

3. Distribute materials. Use Let's Talk About the Story ideas as children complete pictures.

Joshua's Visitor

"Joshua," Mom said, "I have a surprise for you. Amy and her mother are corning over to visit us."

Joshua frowned. "I wish she wouldn't come."

"Why Joshua! I thought you liked to play with Amy," said Mom.

"No, I don't!" Joshua yelled. His chin trembled. His eyes filled with tears. He said, "Amy grabs my toys. She kicks over my blocks. I don't like her!"

When Joshua finished, Mom was quiet. Then she said, "Joshua, it could be that Amy doesn't know how to play with other children. Maybe if you try to be her friend, you can help her know how to play in kind ways."

Josh thought for a minute. He still didn't like Amy. But he sighed. "Oh well, all right!" he said slowly.

Joshua took his blocks out in the yard. He very carefully laid them side by side to build a racetrack for his cars. Joshua zoomed his cars along the track. He was having such a good time that he forgot all about Amy.

Then Joshua saw a car stop in front of the house. Amy and her mother got out of the car. Joshua got angry all over again.

"Hello, Joshua," Amy's mother called as she went into the house.

Amy ran to where Joshua was racing his cars.

"I wanna play!" Amy said.

Joshua sighed. Then he said, "I'm racing my cars." He was about to say, "Here, you can have a car" when Amy reached down and grabbed one of Joshua's cars. She ran away, calling, "I have your race car! Ha!"

Now Joshua was VERY angry! He wanted to catch Amy and grab his race car from her. Then he remembered. Maybe he could help Amy be kind.

Joshua sighed. He said to Amy, "You can play with that car. I have other cars to race."

Amy dropped the car. She walked back to Joshua. "What did you make with your blocks?" she asked.

"I made a racetrack for my cars," Joshua answered.

"Can I build a garage out of your blocks?" Amy asked

"OK. I'll help you," Joshua said. Joshua began to help Amy stack the blocks to build a garage.

When Amy's mother called her to come in and put on a sweater, she wondered, *Will Joshua kick over my garage while I'm gone?* As Amy came back to the yard, she saw that Joshua had not kicked over her garage.

"I thought you'd kick over my garage while I was gone," Amy said. "I like to play with you." Amy began to take the block garage apart. She said, "Let's build another racetrack for your cars."

Let's Talk About the Story

What made Joshua angry? Why didn't Joshua like to play with Amy? When Amy came, what did she do? What did Joshua do? What did Joshua and Amy build?

Who are some of your friends? Sometime it's hard to be kind to friends who aren't kind to us. But the Bible says, "Do good to all people." Let's say this Bible verse together. Repeat Bible verse with children. **We can thank God for friends and ask Him to help us be kind, even when it's hard to do.** Pray briefly.

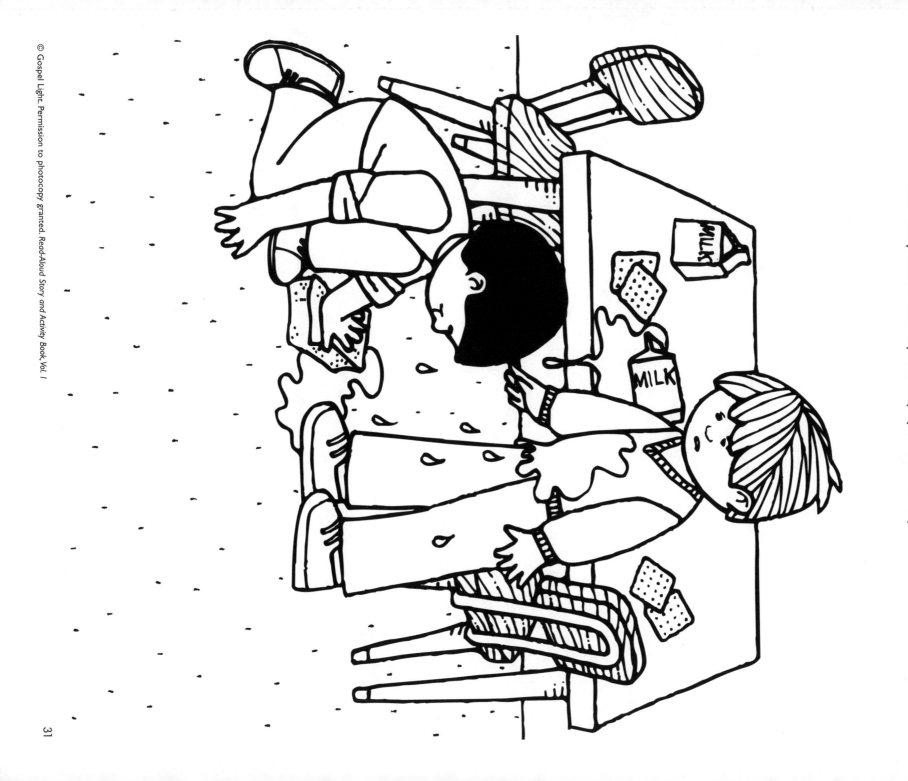

"Be kind to one another." (See Ephesians 4:32.)

Color the picture. Glue a piece of paper towel to Bryce's hand.

Story Picture 13

Read-Aloud Story and Activity

1. Make a copy of Story Picture 13 for yourself and each child. Gather materials; color and complete your copy.
2. **Listen to find out what happened to this boy.** Read story and show completed Story Picture 13.
3. Distribute materials. Use Let's Talk About the Story ideas as children complete pictures.

A Kind Friend

Today Bryce was doing what he liked best in kindergarten—painting. And he was doing his best work. How pretty the yellow and red leaves were!

Jason was painting on the easel next to Bryce. He looked at Bryce's painting. "I'm almost finished," Bryce said. "I want to paint just one more leaf." Jason didn't say anything. He just picked up a brush and slapped a big glob of brown paint in the middle of Bryce's yellow and red leaves.

Bryce was ANGRY. He could feel the tears coming to his eyes. He didn't want to paint anymore. He only felt like ruining Jason's picture. Jason wasn't sad. He was laughing!

Later that morning, during snack time, Jason reached for his graham crackers and knocked over his milk carton. All his milk spilled down the front of his clothes and onto the floor.

Bryce still felt bad about what Jason had done to his painting. When he saw Jason covered in milk, he wanted to laugh. Milk was running down into his shoes. But Bryce saw how sad Jason looked. He knew he should help Jason.

"It's OK, Jason," Bryce said. He brought Jason paper towels and a wet sponge. He helped Jason clean up the milk. When the boys had finished eating, they went to the sandbox and helped build a road. It was fun.

Later Jason said, "I'm sorry I ruined your picture. I won't do it again."

Bryce smiled. "That's OK, Jason," he said. He was glad he had been kind to Jason. It helped Jason want to be kind, even after he had been mean.

Let's Talk About the Story

What did Bryce like to do in kindergarten? What did Jason do? How did Bryce feel? During snack time, what happened to Jason? How did Jason feel? What did Bryce do?

We can show love by being kind when other people need help. Our Bible says, "Be kind to one another." Let's say this Bible verse together. Repeat Bible verse together. **We can pray and ask God to help us always be kind.** Pray briefly.

"God loved us and sent his Son." (See 1 John 4:10.)

Color the picture. Put an **✗** in the box under the tallest tree. Put an **O** in the box under the shortest tree. Draw a tree. Decorate the trees with stars.

Read-Aloud Story and Activity

1. Make a copy of Story Picture 14 for yourself and each child. Gather materials; color and complete your copy.

2. **Listen to find out why a family came to see these trees.** Read story and show completed Story Picture 14.

3. Distribute materials. Use Let's Talk About the Story ideas as children complete pictures.

Which Christmas Tree?

"Daddy, are we almost there?" Anya asked.

"Yes, just a little farther up this road. I promise!" Daddy answered.

Jared and Anya looked out the car window and sang, "We're going to get a Christmas tree. We're getting it today."

Soon Daddy stopped the car. Jared and Anya jumped out and looked up. They looked all around. They were at the Christmas tree lot, all right. Just like Daddy had promised, there were trees EVERYWHERE! Big green trees stood so tall that Jared and Anya almost fell backwards trying to see the tops. Some trees were no taller than Anya. Jared and Anya walked around with Daddy. They looked at every single tree. Tall ones, short ones, skinny ones, full ones—every tree was different. Every tree was beautiful!

Finally Daddy walked over to a middle-sized tree. He touched its full, green branches. He looked at the bottom. He rocked it back and forth a little. Then he said, "This tree looks about right!"

Daddy paid for the tree and tied it onto the back of the car. Jared and Anya climbed in the car and they started home. They'd gotten a tree, like Dad said they would!

"Dad, where did all those trees come from?" Jared asked.

"God made those trees grow in the forest. That man cut the trees and bought them here. And we got a tree, just like I promised we would." Daddy said.

"God made everything—even snow," Anya said as she watched the snowflakes begin to fall. "And God made me, too."

"You're right, Anya," Daddy said. "God made each one of us. The best part is that God LOVES each one of us. And God loved us all SO much, He made a promise, too. He promised to send His Son, Jesus. Jesus came from heaven to show us how very MUCH God loves us. God kept His promise. That's why we have Christmas!"

For a few minutes everyone was still as they rode along. Then Anya said, "God kept His promise to send Jesus like you kept your promise to get the tree! "

Jared said, "Those are good promises!"

Let's Talk About the Story

What did Anya and Jared and their daddy buy? How did they get the tree home? Who made the trees they saw? Who made a promise to Jared and Anya? What promise did God make?

At Christmastime, we remember that God sent Jesus. It's the reason we have Christmas! The Bible says, "God loved us and sent his Son." Let's say this Bible verse together. Repeat Bible verse with children. **We can thank God for keeping His promise. He sent Jesus to show us how much He loves us.** Pray briefly.

"Good news! Today Jesus has been born." (See Luke 2:10,11.)

Color the picture.

Read-Aloud Story and Activity

1. Make a copy of Story Picture 15 for yourself and each child. Gather materials; color and complete your copy.

2. **Listen to find out what game these children played.** Read story and show completed Story Picture 15.

3. Distribute materials. Use Let's Talk About the Story ideas as children complete pictures.

Guess Who!

Mark and Michael were watching TV. They were watching a program about Christmas. The people in the story put shiny balls on a Christmas tree. They made cookies together. They wrapped boxes and boxes full of presents! Then they went outside to ride in a sleigh in the snow. A beautiful horse pulled the sleigh. The people laughed as they rode over the snowy roads.

When the story was over, Dad said. "Time to turn off the TV. Let's play a game together."

Michael jumped into Dad's lap. He said, "Let's play horsey! I want a ride!"

Mark added, "Did you see the horse in the TV story, Dad? It was a big brown horse. It was tall!"

Dad laughed and pulled his boys close. "Yes," he said. "I saw the beautiful horse and the one-horse sleigh, too. That looked like fun."

Mom sat down beside them. She said, "I saw people wrapping lots of presents, too."

Dad said, "I know! Let's play a guessing game. I'm thinking of a kind of gift that didn't come out of a box. It's a gift that couldn't be wrapped up."

"I know!" said Michael "A horsey! You can't wrap a horsey!"

"I know! I know!" said Mark. "A bike! It's too big to wrap, too!"

Dad laughed. He said, "Let me tell you another clue. This gift I am thinking of is a person, not a thing!"

Mom smiled. "And this person was a gift from God!" she added.

Mark and Michael looked at Dad with big eyes. A PERSON that was a gift? A gift that couldn't be wrapped? WHO was a gift that was a person?

Then Mark laughed. "I know!" he said. "It's JESUS! Jesus is the person who came from God. He got born in a stable and there were sheep and angels."

"Were there horses?" asked Michael. "Was Jesus born by the horses?"

Dad pulled his boys close and opened his Bible. "Let's see!" he said. Dad read the story of how Jesus was born. The Bible told about shepherds and sheep. The Bible told about angels, but it didn't mention horses.

Michael looked up at his dad. "Did Jesus ever have a horse? Did He ever ride in a sleigh?"

Mom and Dad smiled. Mom said, "In the place where Jesus was born, there weren't many horses. And there wasn't snow. It was warm."

Dad added, "But Jesus' family loved Him very much, just like Mom and I love you two! God loved Jesus, too. And God loves us! That's why He sent Jesus."

"I'm glad Jesus was born!" said Michael.

"Me, too," said Mark. "They didn't show anything about Jesus on that story on TV."

Mom said, "But Jesus' birth is the whole the reason we have Christmas!"

Dad hugged everyone close. "He sure is. Let's talk to God and tell Him thank You for sending Jesus to us!"

Let's Talk About the Story

What was the story on TV about? What animal pulled the sleigh? What kinds of animals might have been in the stable when Jesus was born? What else does the Bible tell about the time Jesus was born?

We're glad Jesus was born! Our Bible says, "Good news! Today Jesus has been born." It's good to know that Jesus was born. Let's say this Bible verse together. Repeat Bible verse with children. **We can thank God for sending Jesus. And we can tell Him we are glad that Jesus was born!** Pray briefly.

"It is good to give thanks to the Lord." (See Psalm 92:1.)

Connect the dots. Color the picture.

Please come to church with me. Kyle

Story Picture 16

Read-Aloud Story and Activity

1. Make a copy of Story Picture 16 for yourself and each child. Gather materials; color and complete your copy.

2. **Listen to find out what one boy couldn't find.** Read story and show completed Story Picture 16.

3. Distribute materials. Use Let's Talk About the Story ideas as children complete pictures.

The Christmas Card

"Be sure to keep your mittens on, Kyle," Mom said. "It's cold outside."

"I will," Kyle promised. He ran out the door and down the steps. Kyle carried a red card. It was a Christmas card he had made for his friend Ryan.

I hope Ryan can go to church with me, Kyle thought to himself. *I want him to know about Jesus' birthday. I'm glad Jesus was born!*

As Kyle walked toward Ryan's house, he looked at the prints his feet made in the snow. He walked on his tiptoes to make tiny footprints. He hopped with his feet together and made WIDE footprints. Then Kyle kicked the snow high into the air with his toes as he walked. So many kinds of footprints were behind him, he didn't know which ones he liked best!

Suddenly a snowball went ker-splash against Kyle's arm! Kyle looked around. Ryan was hiding behind a bush. Kyle picked up some snow and threw it at his friend.

The boys laughed as they threw snowballs at each other. Then they rolled over and over in the soft cold snow. Finally they were out of breath from laughing and playing so hard. They decided to go to Ryan's house.

Then Kyle remembered! "Where's my card?" he said, looking around. "I dropped it when we were playing."

Kyle and Ryan looked and looked for the red card. Finally Kyle saw something in the snow under a bush. He ran over to the tiny bit of red in the white snow. Kyle pulled at the red corner. He brushed off the snow. Then he handed the card to Ryan. "It's a Christmas invitation. I made it all by myself," Kyle said.

Kyle watched as Ryan opened it. Then Kyle explained, "The card says I want you to come to my church on Christmas. Can you come?"

"OK," answered Ryan. "But I have to ask my mom first."

"Let's ask her now," said Kyle.

The two boys ran into Ryan's house, Ryan showed his mom his pretty invitation. Kyle told her all about Christmas at his church.

"Why, Kyle, how nice! I'm sure Ryan would like to go with you to your church," she said.

"Can he come? Can he come?" Kyle asked.

"Yes, Ryan may go," said Ryan's mom. "Thank you for asking him!"

Ryan and Kyle were so excited, they began to jump up and down. Then they laughed and ran outside to throw more snowballs!

Let's Talk About the Story

What did Kyle make to give Ryan? What happened to the card? Where did Kyle invite Ryan to go? Could Ryan go with Kyle?

Who are some people you like to tell good news to? God wants us to tell others the good news about Jesus. Our Bible says, "It is good to give thanks to the Lord." Let's say this Bible verse together. Repeat Bible verse with children. **We can thank God for Jesus. And we can ask Him to help us tell others the good news about Jesus!** Pray briefly.

"I will praise you, O Lord." 2 Samuel 22:50
Connect the dots. Color the picture.

Story Picture 17

Read-Aloud Story and Activity

1. Make a copy of Story Picture 17 for yourself and each child. Gather materials; color and complete your copy.

2. **Listen to find out what this girl asked about a star.** Read story and show completed Story Picture 17.

3. Distribute materials. Use Let's Talk About the Story ideas as children complete pictures.

A Special Star

"Daddy . . . Daddy," Heather whispered as she tiptoed into the living room one night.

Daddy looked up as Heather came into the room. "Heather, why aren't you in bed—asleep?"

"I WAS asleep, but I woke up again," Heather said.

"Well, come on now. I'll tuck you into bed again," Daddy said. As he pulled up Heather's blanket, Heather whispered, "I can see a big star out my window. I wish I could touch that big star. Maybe if I had a tall, tall ladder . . ."

Daddy laughed quietly. "God placed all the stars in the sky much too far away for us to touch them," he explained.

"Is that big star like the one the wise men saw?" Heather asked.

"I think the star God put in the sky for the wise men was even bigger and brighter than that one," Daddy answered. "God used the big star to tell the wise men something very important. What did the wise men do when they saw the big star?"

"I know! They rode on their camels to see Jesus," Heather answered. Then Heather and Daddy were quiet as they looked at the twinkling stars.

"I wish God would make a star to tell me something special," Heather said.

"Maybe God does make stars to tell us something special. Who made that big bright star we're watching?" Daddy asked.

"God made it," Heather answered.

"Then God uses that star to help you remember He made the stars and put them in the sky."

"What else does the star tell me?" Heather asked.

"It seems to me that the star helps us remember that God made you and me, too." Daddy whispered. "But best of all, the star helps us remember that God loves us very much."

Heather was quiet. She was thinking. *God made all those stars. God made me. AND God loves me—much, much more than ALL the stars.*

"Now, let's go back to sleep," Daddy said. "Tomorrow you can tell Mom all about your special star." Daddy kissed Heather and tiptoed out of the room. Very soon the little girl with a special star was fast asleep.

Let's Talk About the Story

What did Heather wish she could touch? What did Daddy say the stars could help us remember? When you see the stars in our nighttime sky, what can you remember? Who followed the star to see Jesus?

When the wise men came to see Jesus, they praised and thanked God! Our Bible says, "I will praise you, O Lord." Let's say this Bible verse together. Repeat Bible verse with children. **Let's thank God for sending Jesus. God loves us very much.** Pray briefly.

"I will sing of the Lord's great love forever." Psalm 89:1

Draw a line under each of God's wonders you see in the picture. Color the picture.

Story Picture 18

Read-Aloud Story and Activity

1. Make a copy of Story Picture 18 for yourself and each child. Gather materials; color and complete your copy.

2. **Listen to find out what these children are looking for.** Read story and show completed Story Picture 18.

3. Distribute materials. Use Let's Talk About the Story ideas as children complete pictures.

In the Woods

Grandpa slowed the car and parked near the edge of the road. "This looks like a good place," he said.

Ben and Megan were excited! They were going to the woods with Grandpa. It was their first visit since they had been last summer.

Grandpa and Megan and Ben walked along the path into the woods. Grandpa carried their picnic lunch. Megan and Ben went on ahead. "Look for a shady place to eat lunch," Grandpa called to the children.

As they went along the path, Megan skipped. Ben jumped over logs. In a few minutes, Ben came running back. "We found a good place," he said. "It's right by a little stream." Ben led the way.

While they were eating, they watched chipmunks running on the ground. A squirrel hopped in a tree.

"What are the chipmunks and squirrel doing?" asked Megan.

"They're looking for things to eat," said Grandpa. "God loves them. He takes care of them by giving them food to eat. They just have to find it!"

After lunch, Ben and Megan took off their shoes and socks and put their feet into the stream. The water was very cold and they pulled their feet out quickly.

Suddenly Ben said, "Look, Grandpa! I can see some little fish swimming!"

Grandpa came to the edge of the water. He looked through the water and said, "Yes, Ben, but those aren't really fish. They're tadpoles. And we're going to get some to take home!"

Grandpa pulled a jar out of his bag. He scooped the water with the jar and, slosh, there were some little tadpoles in the jar!

"Now we can take them home and watch them grow into frogs," Grandpa said. "It will be fun to see them grow legs and change every day!"

Ben carried the jar part of the way back to the car. Megan carried it part of the way. In the car, they put the jar between them, so they could see. Tadpoles were swimming, right there in the car!

"Grandpa," Ben asked, "Why did God make tadpoles?" he asked.

Grandpa smiled. "God made tadpoles and everything else for us to enjoy! God cares about you and me and everything He has made!"

Let's Talk About the Story

Where did Megan and Ben go? What did Grandpa tell them about the chipmunks? What did Grandpa scoop up for them to bring home?

God cares for us and for all the things He has made! Our Bible says, "I will sing of the Lord's great love forever." Let's say this Bible verse together. Repeat Bible verse with children. **Let's thank God for caring for us. God loves us and cares for everything He has made.** Pray briefly.

"Great is our Lord and mighty in power." Psalm 147:5

Draw Bryson's and Katie's faces to show how they felt after hearing Mom's prayer. Color the picture.

Story Picture 19

Read-Aloud Story and Activity

1. Make a copy of Story Picture 19 for yourself and each child. Gather materials; color and complete your copy.

2. **Listen to find out where this family is going.** Read story and show completed Story Picture 19.

3. Distribute materials. Use Let's Talk About the Story ideas as children complete pictures.

The Rainstorm

"Are the picnic things all in the car?" Mommy asked, as they left the campground.

"Yes," answered Bryson and Katie. They climbed into their seats and fastened their seat belts.

"Thank you for helping," Mommy said. "Now we are ready to go home."

Daddy started the car and soon Bryson and Katie, Mommy and Daddy were riding along the big highway.

"I liked eating in the campground," Katie said.

"I liked playing in the water," said Bryson.

Daddy looked at the sky. "I think we started home just in time. The sky looks as if there's going to be a rainstorm."

The sky grew dark and soon little drops of rain fell pitter-pat on the car windows. Then the raindrops got bigger and bigger until BIG drops of rain were splashing on the windows. The rain fell harder and faster. The wind blew. Lightning streaked across the sky with a CRACK! Then thunder sounded like a big drum. Boom! Rrrumble. BOOM!

"I don't like that loud noise," Bryson said. He put his hands over his ears. Katie covered her eyes with her hands as lightning flashed across the sky. "I'm scared!" Katie said. She began to cry.

Mommy turned and patted Bryson and Katie. "You don't have to be afraid," she said. "God knows all about this rainstorm. And God cares about you."

Mommy quietly said, "Thank You, God, for caring about Bryson and Katie. Thank You that You know about the storm. Thank You that You are here to help us. In Jesus' name, amen."

Both children began to smile just a little. And it wasn't long before the thunder and lightning stopped. The rain began to fall with a gentle pitter-pat pitter-pat on the windows again.

"I see blue sky," Bryson said. "The clouds are going away."

"I think the storm is over," said Daddy.

"I'm glad God cares about us," said Bryson.

Let's Talk About the Story

Where had Katie and Bryson, Mommy and Daddy been? What happened on the way home? When Bryson heard the thunder, what did he do? When Katie saw the lightning, what did she do? What did Mommy do? Have you ever been in a storm? How did you feel?

God cares for us. Even in storms, He is taking care of us! Our Bible says, "Great is our Lord and mighty in power." Let's say this Bible verse together. Repeat Bible verse with children. **Let's thank God for caring for us. He loves us and cares for us, even when we are afraid.** Pray briefly.

"The Lord is good to all." Psalm 145:9
Draw Grandma's glasses where Kristy found them.
Connect the dots. Glue fabric scrap to blanket. Color the picture.

Read-Aloud Story and Activity

1. Make a copy of Story Picture 20 for yourself and each child. Gather materials; color and complete your copy.

2. **Listen to find out what this grandma is looking for.** Read story and show completed Story Picture 20.

3. Distribute materials. Use Let's Talk About the Story ideas as children complete pictures.

Grandma's Glasses

"Grandma's here! Grandma's here!" Seth shouted. Grandma came into the house and gave Seth a big hug.

"Me, too," said little Kristy. So Grandma gave Kristy a big hug, too.

Seth said, "I love you, Grandma. You do lots of things for me."

"That's because I love you," Grandma said.

Mom came into the room. She whispered to Seth, "If you watch, you will find ways to show your love for Grandma while she visits us."

"What can I do to help her?" Seth whispered back.

"Grandma gets tired easily. She needs to go rest now. You can help by being quiet," Mom answered.

"Oh, there goes Kristy past Grandma's door with her noisy, quackity pull-toy!" said Seth. Quickly he took Kristy's hand and played Peekaboo with her on the back porch.

"See what I mean?" Mom said. "You showed your love for Grandma by helping Kristy play quietly."

The next day while Grandma was dusting, Seth said, "Here, Grandma, let me dust the low things. You can dust the high things that I can't reach yet."

"Oh, thank you, Seth!" said Grandma, smiling. "That's a good way to help."

That evening at bedtime, Grandma said, "It's story time! But I can't find my glasses!"

"I'll help you find them," Seth said.

"I'll help, too." Kristy said.

So Grandma looked in all the high places. No glasses! Seth and Kristy looked in all the low places. No glasses! Then Grandma sighed. She was sad. She said, "I just can't see well enough to read without my glasses."

"That's all right," said Seth. "I'll tell about the pictures in my Bible storybook." Kristy sat on Grandma's lap. Seth told about all the pictures!

Then it was Kristy's bedtime. Grandma carried her to bed and bent down to give her a good-night kiss. "Grandma's glasses!" Kristy said, as she patted Grandma's head. Sure enough! There were Grandma's glasses! They were on her head the whole time! Grandma sat down and laughed.

Later Seth said, "Grandma, now that you have your glasses, will you read me a story?" Guess what story Seth chose? He chose the Bible story about the blind man that Jesus helped to see.

Let's Talk About the Story

What are ways Seth showed his love for Grandma? Who dusted the low things? The high things? What did Grandma lose? Who found them? Where were Grandma's glasses? Seth and Kristy helped their grandma! Seth and Kristy knew their grandma loved them.

We can see many ways Jesus shows His love to us. Our Bible says, "The Lord is good to all." Let's say this Bible verse together. Repeat Bible verse with children. **What are some ways Jesus shows His love for us? Let's thank God for the many ways Jesus shows His love.** Pray briefly.

"God gives us what we need." (See Philippians 4:19.)
Count the sheep. Count the birds. Connect the dots.
Glue cotton balls on sheep. Color the picture.

Story Picture 21

Read-Aloud Story and Activity

1. Make a copy of Story Picture 21 for yourself and each child. Gather materials; color and complete your copy.

2. **Listen to find out what a boy saw.** Read story and show completed Story Picture 21.

3. Distribute materials. Use Let's Talk About the Story ideas as children complete pictures.

Winter Clothes

"Don't go so fast, Daddy," Sam said as he and his family rode along in the country. "I want to see those woolly sheep! Last time we saw them, they were so skinny!"

"The sheep looked skinny last time because the farmer had cut off all their wool," Daddy said. He slowed down as he drove past the sheep.

"Did it hurt?" Sam wanted to know.

"Does it hurt when you get your hair cut?" Daddy asked.

"No," Sam answered, "but sometimes it tickles."

Daddy laughed. "Maybe it tickles the sheep, too, but it doesn't hurt. The farmer sells the wool to a man who makes it into cloth. The wool cloth is made into warm clothing for people to wear when the weather gets cold."

"Your sweater is made of wool," added Mom.

Ashley sat quietly listening to Daddy and Sam. Finally she said, "If the farmer cuts off the sheep's wool, how does the sheep stay warm in the winter?"

"God planned for the sheep's wool to grow back again, so the sheep will be warm," Daddy answered. "That's why the sheep look so big and fat now. Their wool has grown back."

"Does our dog, Tippy, have wool to keep him warm?" Ashley asked.

"Tippy has fur, not wool," Daddy answered. "But God planned a way

for Tippy to stay warm, too. Tippy's fur grows thicker when the weather starts to get cold. In winter, he has a thicker fur coat. It keeps him warm."

"Look at what is sitting on that post," Mom pointed out the window.

"A bird!" Sam said.

"What kind of clothing did God plan for him?" Mom asked.

"I know," Ashley answered. "Feathers!"

"That's right," Mom said. "When it was hot last summer, many of the bird's feathers dropped out. When it got cold, the bird grew new feathers. Now he has a warm feather coat."

"It looks like God knows just the right kind of clothes for each of us," Daddy said. "God gives us all sorts of good things!"

Let's Talk About the Story

Why did the sheep look skinny last time Sam saw them? What happened to the sheep's wool? What kind of coat did God plan for a dog? For a bird?

We can thank Jesus for His love and the good things He gives us. Our Bible says, "God gives us what we need." **Let's say this Bible verse together.** Repeat Bible verse with children. **Let's thank Jesus for the many ways He shows His love and the good things He gives us.** Pray briefly.

"Be kind to everyone." 2 Timothy 2:24

Color the picture.

Read-Aloud Story and Activity

1. Make a copy of Story Picture 22 for yourself and each child. Gather materials; color and complete your copy.

2. **Listen to find out how these children solved a problem.** Read story and show completed Story Picture 22.

3. Distribute materials. Use Let's Talk About the Story ideas as children complete pictures.

ME First!

"I'm first!" said Dylan. "You're always first!" Dylan tightly held the new box of crayons. Maria wasn't going to be FIRST this time! Dylan wanted to use those new, sharp crayons before anyone else.

"ME FIRST!" shouted Maria. She grabbed the crayon box as hard as SHE could, too. Dylan tugged the crayon box. Maria held on and wouldn't let go.

Aunt Elena came into the room. "What's the matter?" she asked.

Dylan shouted, "Maria ALWAYS takes the crayons first! I want to be first!"

Gently Aunt Elena put her hands on the crayon box. Now THREE people were holding onto it! She said, "I can see that both of you want the crayons first. You can fight and be angry or you can find a way to share. Can you think of a way to solve your problem?"

Dylan frowned. He took a deep breath. Then he looked at Maria. "Maybe we could count the crayons. You get half."

Maria frowned. She took a deep breath. Then she sighed. "OK," she said. Then she added, "I'm sorry."

Dylan smiled a little smile. "That's OK," he said. "I forgive you. And I'm sorry, too."

"I forgive you, too," smiled Maria. "Let's count the crayons. Then we both have new crayons to use!"

Dylan and Maria sat down at the table. They opened the box of crayons and saw that inside were four little boxes of crayons.

"Look!" said Dylan. "Two for me and two for you!"

Maria laughed, "THAT was easy counting!"

Dylan and Maria found some paper. They drew pictures with the new crayons—tiny lines, fat lines, bright new colors! When one of Maria's red crayons broke, Dylan found another red one.

"Here," he said, "try this one! I have another reddish one."

Aunt Elena looked into the room. "I'm glad you forgave each other!" she said. "That's how we show God's love to each other!"

Let's Talk About the Story

Why were Dylan and Maria fighting? What did Aunt Elena say they could do? How were Dylan and Maria kind to each other? How did they solve their problem?

Sometimes it's hard to forgive. But forgiving is a way to show God's love. God will help us forgive and be kind. Our Bible says, "Be kind to everyone." Let's say this Bible verse together. Repeat Bible verse with children. **We can ask God to help us forgive each other and be kind instead of fighting.** Pray briefly.

"Jesus said, 'Love each other.'" (See John 15:17.)

Color the picture. Glue a folded piece of newspaper where Luke found Mrs. Brown's newspaper.

Story Picture 23

Read-Aloud Story and Activity

1. Make a copy of Story Picture 23 for yourself and each child. Gather materials; color and complete your copy.

2. **Listen to find out what this lady is looking for.** Read story and show completed Story Picture 23.

3. Distribute materials. Use Let's Talk About the Story ideas as children complete pictures.

Mrs. Brown's Helpers

"Race you to the corner!" Luke said to Sara as he ran down the sidewalk. And sure enough, Luke got to the corner first.

"But I can run faster on the way back," Sara said. And off she started as fast as she could run. Luke almost caught up with her as they came to their yard. They sat down on the porch steps to rest a minute.

Just then their neighbor Mrs. Brown came out of her front door. Mrs. Brown looked on her porch. She looked on her steps. She went down the steps and looked in her yard.

"What's Mrs. Brown doing?" Sara wondered.

"She's looking for something," Luke whispered.

"Let's go see if we can help her," Sara said.

"Hello there!" Mrs. Brown said as Luke and Sara came into her yard.

"What are you looking for?" Sara asked.

"I'm looking for my newspaper," Mrs. Brown answered.

We came to help you look," Luke said.

"Good! I need someone to help me look," Mrs. Brown smiled. Luke and Sara looked for the newspaper under the bushes. They looked behind the trees. They looked in the driveway. But no newspaper did they find—until Luke saw something white.

"There's your newspaper, Mrs. Brown," he said. "It's caught up there—in that big bush." Mrs. Brown and Sara looked up where Luke was pointing. Sure enough, there was the newspaper near the top of the highest bush.

"Oh, dear. I can't quite reach it," Mrs. Brown said, reaching as high as she could. Then Sara had an idea. "Hold me up and I'll reach it for you," Sara said.

And that is just what Mrs. Brown did. She held Sara up as high as she could. Sara easily reached the newspaper. "Here it is!" said Sara as she handed the paper to Mrs. Brown.

"Well, thank you both for your kind help. Luke, you found the paper. And Sara, you reached it for me. Thanks so much!" Mrs. Brown smiled.

Luke and Sara ran back home. "Let's take our own newspaper into the house and surprise Mommy," said Luke. And that is just what these two kind helpers did!

Let's Talk About the Story

What was Mrs. Brown looking for? What did Luke and Sara do to help Mrs. Brown? Why do you think they wanted to help her? How were Luke and Sara kind to their mother?

We show God's love to other people by helping them when they need help. Our Bible says, "Jesus said, 'Love each other.'" Let's say this Bible verse together. Repeat Bible verse with children. **Let's think of some ways we can help people who need our help. Now let's ask God to help us do those things!** Pray briefly.

"Forgive each other." (See Colossians 3:13.)

Connect the dots. Color the pictures. Fold Scene 3 over Scene 2. Fold Scene 1 back. Show scenes as story action indicates.

FOLD

FOLD

SCENE 1

SCENE 2

SCENE 3

Story Picture 25

Read-Aloud Story and Activity

1. Make a copy of Story Picture 25 for yourself and each child. Gather materials; color and complete your copy.

2. **Listen to find out what happened in this family.** Read story and show completed Story Picture 25.

3. Distribute materials. Use Let's Talk About the Story ideas as children complete pictures.

Micah Is Sorry

Micah sat on the back step. He was sad—and angry, too. *Amy played with my truck and broke off a wheel. Now it won't roll,* Micah thought. Micah knew Amy hadn't meant to break his truck. It had been an accident. *Mom said Daddy could fix it. But Daddy won't be home till dinnertime,* Micah thought. The more he thought, the angrier he felt.

Then Micah went into the house. He didn't see Amy. Quietly he went into Amy's room. He looked all around. There was Amy's favorite doll. He picked it up. Then he pulled on the doll. He pulled until one arm tore off. He was a little surprised. NOW what should he do with the doll? Micah threw it on the floor. He kicked it partway under the bed. He turned and went back to sit on the porch steps.

Micah thought he would be happy after he had broken Amy's doll. But instead, he felt worse than he did before. Big tears came up in Micah's eyes. He wished he had not torn the arm off Amy's doll. Micah was sorry.

Micah knew there was just one way to make things right again. He told God that he was sorry he had broken Amy's doll. He asked God to forgive him for doing such an unkind thing. Of course God forgave Micah, because God loved him. Micah felt better after he told God he was sorry.

Then Micah went into the house and told Mom what he had done.

"I'm sorry you broke Amy's doll," Mom said. "Let's see if we can fix it."

Micah went back to Amy's room. He picked up the doll from the floor and brought it to Mom.

"I think this will work," Mother said. She got a needle and thread and she sewed the arm back in place.

Just then Amy came into the room. She looked at Mom and then at Micah. She looked angry. "What are you doing with my doll?" she asked.

"Mom's fixing your doll's arm," Micah said.

"What HAPPENED?" Amy wanted to know.

Micah said quietly, "I pulled it off. I was mad because you broke the wheel off my truck." Micah stopped. Then he said, "I'm sorry, Amy."

Amy looked at her brother. She could see Micah WAS really sorry.

"I'm sad that you broke my doll. But I forgive you," Amy said. Then they heard a car come in the driveway.

"That's Daddy!" Micah said. "Now he can fix my truck!"

Let's Talk About the Story

What did Micah do to Amy's doll? After he broke the doll, how did he feel? What did he say to God in his prayer? How did Mom help? What did Amy do?

When we forgive the people in our families, we are showing God's love. Our Bible says, "Forgive each other." Let's say this Bible verse together. Repeat Bible verse with children. **We can ask God to help us forgive and be kind to the people in our families!** Pray briefly.

"Serve one another in love." Galatians 5:13

Connect the dots. Color the picture.

Story Picture 26

Read-Aloud Story and Activity

1. Make a copy of Story Picture 26 for yourself and each child. Gather materials; color and complete your copy.

2. **Listen to find out why this family is in the airport.** Read story and show completed Story Picture 26.

3. Distribute materials. Use Let's Talk About the Story ideas as children complete pictures.

Aunt Linda's Visit

"Look at all the airplanes!" Michael shouted. Mom, Dad, Michael and Lauren were at the airport to pick up Aunt Linda. She was coming to visit.

Lauren put her hands over her ears as a big jet came in for a landing. "Is that the plane Aunt Linda is on?" Michael asked.

"I think so!" Dad answered.

"Let's hurry!" Michael said. "I want to meet her!" He grabbed Dad's hand and ran into the airport.

They found the gate where Aunt Linda would be arriving. They looked for Aunt Linda as the people got off the plane.

"There is Aunt Linda!" Lauren shouted, jumping up and down. Aunt Linda came over and gave everyone a "hello" hug. They began walking to the baggage claim area.

Michael thought a minute. He wanted Aunt Linda to know he was GLAD she was here to visit, so he asked, "Aunt Linda, may I carry your little bag?"

"Sure!" said Aunt Linda. Michael picked up her bag and walked beside Dad. Dad was carrying a big suitcase.

"I want to help, too! Aunt Linda, how can I help you?" Lauren asked.

"You may carry my sweater," Aunt Linda said. She handed it to Lauren. Lauren carried the sweater very carefully! She never let it drag on the ground.

When they got to the car, Michael started to get in. Then he stopped. "You get in first, Aunt Linda," he said.

Aunt Linda smiled. "Thank you," she said. "You and Lauren are very good helpers!"

The next morning after breakfast, Lauren went outside to play. Then she remembered she wanted to show Aunt Linda her kittens. She went back into the kitchen. "Aunt Linda," she said, "I want to show—" Lauren stopped. Mom and Aunt Linda were still talking. Lauren wanted her aunt to come right away, but she waited until Aunt Linda and Mom had finished talking. Then she said, "Could you come and see the kittens?"

Aunt Linda got up from the table and followed Lauren to the porch where the baby kittens were playing in their box. "They're the prettiest kittens I've ever seen!" said Aunt Linda.

Lauren was glad her aunt had come to visit. And she was glad she and Michael could be good helpers!

Let's Talk About the Story

Where did Michael and Lauren and their parents go to pick up Aunt Linda? What kind things did Michael and Lauren do for Aunt Linda? What kind things do you do for people?

Jesus tells us to be kind and to serve, or help, each other. Our Bible says, "Serve one another in love." Let's say this Bible verse together. Repeat Bible verse with children. **Let's pray. We can ask God to help us serve and help each other!** Pray briefly.

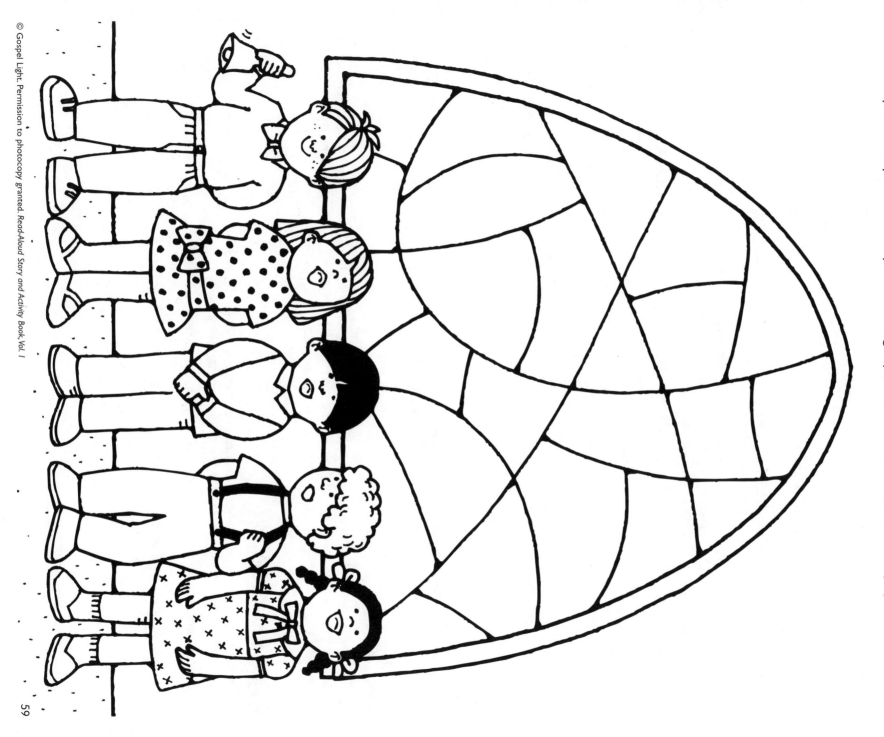

"Sing praises to the Lord." Psalm 9:11

Color the picture. (Optional: Glue pieces of brightly colored tissue or construction paper on window.)

Read-Aloud Story and Activity

1. Make a copy of Story Picture 27 for yourself and each child. Gather materials; color and complete your copy.

2. **Listen to find out why one boy isn't singing.** Read story and show completed Story Picture 27.

3. Distribute materials. Use Let's Talk About the Story ideas as children complete pictures.

Branden's Lost Voice

"Guess what!" Anna said as she ran into Branden's bedroom. Anna had just gotten home from church. "We're going to sing a song in the grown-ups' church next week!"

Branden was sitting up in bed. He had just had his tonsils out and his throat felt sore. Branden smiled at Anna's good news. Singing in the big church sounded exciting! Then his face suddenly looked sad. He pointed to his throat and said in a strange little whisper, "I can't sing. I can't even talk."

Anna looked sad, too. Then she said, "Maybe you'll be all better by next week." Anna ran to the living room.

"I think Branden might feel better by next week," said Mom. "We'll just have to wait and see. Right now you may take him some ice cream." Mom and Anna went out to the kitchen. Mom scooped some vanilla ice cream into a dish. Anna carried the dish of ice cream into the bedroom. How good it tasted to Branden! It felt nice and cold sliding down his throat.

Afterward, Anna opened her storybook with the pictures in it. "I'll tell you about the pictures," she said.

Then she said, "I'll sing you the song we are going to sing in the big church." As Anna sang, Branden tried to sing along. But he couldn't make a sound!

During the days that followed, Branden's throat began to feel better. By the middle of the week, he could talk a little again in his own voice. But when he tried to sing, he just couldn't! How would he be able to sing in the big church?

On the big day, the children in Mrs. Lee's class were excited and happy. All but Branden! He still couldn't sing! Then Mrs. Lee said, "I have a surprise for Branden," and she opened her Bible. "Our Bible says to make a joyful sound to the Lord." Mrs. Lee opened a red box. She lifted out a pretty bell and rang it. "And Branden can use this bell to make a joyful sound while we sing." Branden smiled as Mrs. Lee gave him the bell and showed him how to ring it.

The big church was full of pretty flowers and smiling faces! Branden held the bell very carefully. He rang the bell as the children sang their song of praise to the Lord. He forgot all about being sad that he couldn't sing. He was glad he could ring the bell. He could praise Jesus and show he loved Him!

Let's Talk About the Story

Why couldn't Branden sing? What was Mrs. Lee's surprise? What did Branden do to make a joyful sound to the Lord? How did Branden feel when the children sang their song?

We can praise Jesus and show our love for Him. Our Bible says, "Sing praises to the Lord." Let's say this Bible verse together. Repeat Bible verse with children. **Let's thank God that we can sing and ring bells and do many other things to praise Jesus and show we love Him!** Pray briefly.

"It is true! The Lord has risen." Luke 24:34

Color the ✗ spaces brown. Color the ○ spaces red. Color the △ spaces blue.

Story Picture 28

Read-Aloud Story and Activity

1. Make a copy of Story Picture 28 for yourself and each child. Gather materials; color and complete your copy.

2. **Listen to find out what Lauren was looking for.** Read story and show completed Story Picture 28.

3. Distribute materials. Use Let's Talk About the Story ideas as children complete pictures.

Something New for Eastertime

"Ginger! Ginger!" Lauren called to her cat. But Ginger didn't come. *Where could she be?*

"Mother, may I go look for Ginger?" Lauren asked.

"Yes," Mother answered.

Out the door Lauren ran calling, "Ginger! Ginger!" As she came to the house next door, Lauren saw Mr. Clark painting his fence.

"Good morning," Lauren said. "Why are you painting your fence?"

"It's spring!" answered Mr. Clark. "Eastertime is coming. Don't you think my flowers will look pretty against a fresh white fence?"

"Oh, yes," said Lauren. "I like spring. I'm glad Eastertime is coming. Mr. Clark, did you see my cat?"

"No, I haven't seen her," Mr. Clark answered. So Lauren walked on a little further. She saw Mrs. Jones on a ladder, washing her windows.

"Good morning!" Lauren called. "Why are you washing your windows?"

"I'm doing my spring cleaning!" answered Mrs. Jones. "I want my house to be nice and clean for Eastertime."

"I'm glad it's almost Eastertime," Lauren said. "Did you see my cat, Ginger?" Mrs. Jones hadn't seen Ginger either. So Lauren walked on. Mr. Miller was digging around some plants in his flower garden.

"Good morning, Mr. Miller," Lauren said. "What are you doing?"

"I'm pulling weeds from our flower garden," answered Mr. Miller. "It's spring. These white lilies will be ready to bloom for Eastertime."

Mrs. Miller was sitting on the porch. She was sewing a pretty dress for her daughter, Kim. "Good morning," Lauren said. "What are you making?"

"This is Kim's new dress," answered Mrs. Miller. "We like to wear pretty new things at Eastertime to show we are happy that Jesus is living."

"I have a yellow dress and new white shoes to wear," Lauren said.

Just then the phone rang in the house. Mrs. Miller went inside to answer it. "Lauren, that was your mother," Mrs. Miller said. "She wants you to hurry home for a big surprise."

Lauren ran home as fast as she could. The garage door was open and Mother stood there, smiling. "Come quietly! See what I just found in this box!" Mother said. Lauren looked inside the box.

"Ginger! It's Ginger!" she whispered. "And some baby kittens!" Lauren gently patted her cat. "Oh, Ginger, now you have something new for Eastertime, too."

Let's Talk About the Story

Who was Lauren looking for? Why was Mr. Clark painting his fence? Mrs. Jones washing her windows? Mr. Miller working in his flower garden? Who found Ginger? Where was she? What was the surprise?

We are glad Jesus is alive. We are glad He loves us. Our Bible says, "It is true! The Lord has risen." Let's say this Bible verse together. Repeat Bible verse with children. **We can show our love for Jesus and thank God that Jesus is alive!** Pray briefly.

"Thomas said to Jesus, 'My Lord and my God!' " (See John 20:28.)

Thomas saw that Jesus was alive and he was glad. When we see what God has made, we're glad, too.
Draw the parts of the picture that are missing. Color the picture.

Story Picture 29

Read-Aloud Story and Activity

1. Make a copy of Story Picture 29 for yourself and each child. Gather materials; color and complete your copy.

2. **Listen to find out what game these children are playing.** Read story and show completed Story Picture 29.

3. Distribute materials. Use Let's Talk About the Story ideas as children complete pictures.

The Guessing Game

Dad walked along through the park. Travis and Shannon ran ahead.

"Let's pretend we are birds," Travis called to Shannon. Travis ran, stretching out his arms wide. The wind felt good on his face.

"I like flying!" laughed Shannon. She waved her arms.

"I'm going to sit here," Dad called to Travis and Shannon. Soon Travis and Shannon were tired of being birds. They came to rest by Dad on the bench.

"Let's play a game. Let's see how many things we can find that God has made. We'll take turns guessing," said Dad. "First, guess what I see. I'm looking at something big and tall that God has made. It is green and brown."

"I know," Travis shouted. "It's a tree!"

"You're right," Dad answered. "Now it's your turn to see something God has made. Shannon and I will try to guess what you see."

"I see something green and soft on the ground." Dad and Shannon looked around and tried to guess.

"It's grass! I guessed it!" Shannon shouted. "Now it's my turn." Shannon looked around to see something God made. Then she said, "I see something moving in a tree. It's looking at me."

"Is it a bird?" Travis guessed.

"No, it's not a bird," Shannon laughed.

Travis and Dad looked up into the tree. Then Travis shouted as he pointed to a high branch, "I see it! It's a little squirrel."

"You guessed right!" Shannon said.

Travis and Shannon and Dad had fun looking for things God made! Travis saw some big rocks by the path. Dad saw a little green bug. When it was Shannon's turn, she said, "I'm thinking of something God made that NOBODY can see."

Travis and Dad thought and thought. Finally Shannon had to tell them. "It's the wind!"

"Of course!" Dad said. "I didn't think of the wind!"

Let's Talk About the Story

Where did Travis and Shannon go with Dad? What did they do there? What did they see? What did Shannon think of that Travis and Dad could not guess?

When Thomas didn't see Jesus, he had a hard time believing Jesus is alive. But here is what he said when he saw Jesus. Our Bible tells us, "Thomas said to Jesus, 'My Lord and my God!'" Let's say this Bible verse together. Repeat Bible verse with children. Thomas was glad to see that Jesus is alive. We can tell others this good news, too! Let's thank God that Jesus is alive. Pray briefly.

"Jesus said, 'I am with you always.'" (See Matthew 28:20.)

Find the circles. Find the triangles. Find the squares. Color the picture.

SPACE SHIP

Story Picture 30

Read-Aloud Story and Activity

1. Make a copy of Story Picture 30 for yourself and each child. Gather materials; color and complete your copy.

2. **Listen to find out what this boy is doing.** Read story and show completed Story Picture 30.

3. Distribute materials. Use Let's Talk About the Story ideas as children complete pictures.

Anthony's Spaceship

One day when Mom and Anthony came home from the store, Anthony ran to find his dad. "Daddy! Daddy!" he called all out of breath. "I bought a spaceship. Please help me put it together! I want to fly it to the moon!"

"That's pretty far for a first trip!" laughed Daddy. "Let's put it together. We'll see how far it will fly."

Anthony and Daddy laid out all the parts on the table. They snapped together all the pieces of the spaceship. They placed the nose cone on the front. Then they attached a heavy rubber band to the launcher. "All set!" said Daddy.

Outside, Anthony pulled the spaceship back on the launcher as hard as he could while Daddy started the countdown. "5-4-3-2-1, blast off!" he shouted, and Anthony let go. Zzzzzzzzooooooooooommmmmmmmmm! went the spaceship. Up, up and over a little tree. But the spaceship did not go to the moon.

Anthony tried again. "5-4-3-2-1, blast off!" Zzzzzzzooooooommmm! went the spaceship. Up, up, up, up and over the garage. But it did not go to the moon.

"You try it, Daddy," Anthony said. "5-4-3-2-1, blast off!" Zzzzzzooooooommmmmmm! The spaceship shot straight UP, UP, UP and disappeared over the house next door.

"Maybe it went to the moon!" Anthony shouted.

"I don't think it's quite that big a rocket," Daddy said. "The moon is VERY far away. Only a REAL spaceship can fly to the moon."

Then Anthony asked, "Will we go in a real spaceship when we go up to heaven?"

"No," Daddy answered. "Even the biggest and most powerful spaceship can't take us where heaven is!"

"How will we go then?" Anthony asked.

"Remember how Jesus went to heaven?" Daddy asked.

"Jesus went up, up, up," Anthony said, "right through the clouds. Is that how we'll go?"

"That was a very special way," Daddy said. "When we go to heaven, we will go in a very special way, too. God has a wonderful plan to bring us to heaven with Him. But only God knows exactly how or when we'll go to be with Him in heaven."

Let's Talk About the Story

What did Anthony buy? Where did his spaceship fly? Did it fly to the moon? Why not? What did Daddy say about going to heaven?

When Jesus went back to heaven, He went in a special way. Our Bible tells us, "Jesus said, 'I am with you always.'" Let's say this Bible verse together. Repeat Bible verse with children. **Let's thank God that Jesus is always with us.** Pray briefly.

"Hear the word of God and obey it." Luke 11:28

Fold page to show Scene 1. Draw Megan's face to show how she felt about not obeying. Color the picture.

Fold page to show Scene 2. Draw Megan's face to show how she felt after she told God and her mom she was sorry. Color the picture

FOLD

SCENE 1

SCENE 2

Story Picture 31

Read-Aloud Story and Activity

1. Make a copy of Story Picture 31 for yourself and each child. Gather materials; color and complete your copy.

2. **Listen to find out what happened to this girl.** Read story and show completed Story Picture 31.

3. Distribute materials. Use Let's Talk About the Story ideas as children complete pictures.

Megan Is Sorry

"Good-bye, Mrs. Martin," called Megan. The children were going home from kindergarten. Mrs. Martin waved. "Good-bye, Megan. I'll see you tomorrow."

Megan started to walk down the street. She was glad she was big enough to walk home from kindergarten alone.

"Megan, Megan. Wait for me," a voice called.

Megan's friend Molly was running to catch up with her. Together the two girls walked down the street.

"I got a new dollhouse and some new furniture for it last night," said Molly. "Come to my house and I'll show it to you."

"I have to go straight home after kindergarten," Megan said.

Molly said. "It will only take a minute. I just want to show it to you."

"OK,"' Megan said, "but I can't stay."

Molly brought the new dollhouse and the new furniture to the backyard. Then she brought her dolls out to the dollhouse. Megan and Molly were having fun playing when Megan realized she had been there a long time.

"I have to go home!" Megan said. She picked up her sweater and ran down the street. When she got home, her mom was gone and the house was locked. She sat down on the front steps. *I wonder where Mom is,* she thought.

Soon Mom came up the walk. She was frowning. "Megan, where have you been?" she asked.

"I stopped at Molly's house to see her new dollhouse and furniture," Megan answered.

Mom sat down next to Megan. "You're supposed to come straight home from kindergarten, Megan," she said. "When you didn't come home, I thought something had happened to you. I was out looking for you. You didn't obey."

They went into the house. Megan sat in her bedroom while Mom fixed lunch. She thought about what Mom had said. She knew she hadn't obeyed, and she was sorry. She wanted to obey her mom. She knew Jesus wanted her to obey, too.

Megan prayed, "Dear God, I'm sorry I didn't obey. Help me do what Mom says. In Jesus' name, amen."

Then Megan went to the kitchen. She put her arms around Mom. "I'm sorry I didn't come straight home."

Mom gave Megan a hug. "I forgive you, Megan," said Mom. "I know you'll remember next time." Together they sat down to eat lunch. Mom thanked God for the food and for her girl who wanted to obey!

Let's Talk About the Story

Where did Megan go after kindergarten was over? Why did she stop at Molly's house? Why was Megan's mom looking for her? Because Megan was sorry, what did she do?

Our Bible says, "Hear the word of God and obey it." Let's say this Bible verse together. Repeat Bible verse with children. **Let's thank God that He will help us obey.** Pray briefly.

"Share with God's people who are in need." Romans 12:13

Color the picture. Fold flap forward on dotted line. Unfold flap to show what happened to Natalie's ice cream.

Story Picture 32

FOLD

Read-Aloud Story and Activity

1. Make a copy of Story Picture 32 for yourself and each child. Gather materials; color and complete your copy.

2. **Listen to find out what happened to this ice cream cone.** Read story and show completed Story Picture 32.

3. Distribute materials. Use Let's Talk About the Story ideas as children complete pictures.

Ice Cream Cones

Natalie and Connor sat on the front steps of their house, waiting for their mother to call them.

"I wish Mom would hurry up and finish talking on the phone," Natalie said.

"Mom promised us ice cream cones," Connor said. "I'm going to have a strawberry one."

"I'm going to have peppermint," said Natalie.

Soon they heard their mother coming. "Can we have our ice cream cones now?" Connor asked.

"You certainly may. Both of you have waited very quietly while I talked on the phone," Mom said. "Thank you. I think people who do such a good job waiting should have double-decker ice cream cones."

"Boy, oh, boy! Double-deckers!" Connor shouted. "I want strawberry and chocolate!"

"And I want peppermint and vanilla!" Natalie told Mom.

Mom said, "You both sit right here on the step. And I will bring you the cones."

Soon Mom was back with two BIG ice cream cones and some napkins.

"Thank you, Mom," Connor said. He started to lick his cone. "Mmmmmmmm! This ice cream tastes good!"

"I like peppermint best," Natalie said as she turned her cone to lick the dribbles. Just then a little breeze blew the napkin from her hand. As she reached to grab the napkin, she dropped her ice cream on the ground. Natalie stared with her mouth open. Only her CONE was left!

Natalie began to cry. "Oh, I dropped my ice cream!"

"You can have some of mine," Connor said. He called Mom. She came out with a spoon. Carefully she put some of Connor's strawberry ice cream in Natalie's empty cone. Then they both gave their cones a great big lick and smiled.

"Thank you for the ice cream," Natalie told Connor. Natalie looked down at the ground. "Where is the ice cream that I dropped?" she asked in surprise.

Connor looked. Mom looked, too. All they could see was a wet spot on the ground—and their dog Pippin wagging her tail happily!

"I guess Pippin is the only one who got two kinds of ice cream," laughed Connor.

Let's Talk About the Story

What had Mom promised Connor and Natalie? What kinds of ice cream did Connor want? What kinds did Natalie want? What happened to Natalie's ice cream? What did Connor do? Who ate the ice cream Natalie dropped?

Our Bible says, "Share with God's people who are in need." Let's say this Bible verse together. Repeat Bible verse with children. **Let's pray and ask God to help us share.** Pray briefly.

"Be kind to the poor and you will be happy." (See Proverbs 14:21.)

Draw what Aaron and Nicki put in the wagon. Find the circles in the picture. Color the picture.

Story Picture 33

Read-Aloud Story and Activity

1. Make a copy of Story Picture 33 for yourself and each child. Gather materials; color and complete your copy.

2. **Listen to find out where this family is going.** Read story and show completed Story Picture 33.

3. Distribute materials. Use Let's Talk About the Story ideas as children complete pictures.

Sharing Soup

"Mmm! This is good soup!" Aaron said as he and Nicki were eating their lunch.

"Chicken noodle is my favorite kind," Nicki said. She handed her empty bowl to Mom for more soup.

"I'm glad you like soup," Mom said. "But I know some boys and girls who do not have any lunch today."

"Why don't they eat lunch?" Aaron wanted to know.

"Because their mommies and daddies do not have enough money to buy food," Mom answered.

"I'll give them some of my soup," Nicki suggested.

"Could we do that?" Aaron asked.

Mom was quiet a minute. Then she said, "Yes, I think we can. Maybe some of our neighbors would like to help, too."

After lunch Mom talked on the phone to several people. Then she called, "Nicki! Aaron! Come here."

Nicki and Aaron came quickly to hear Mom's news.

"Lots of our neighbors want to give cans of soup to children who do not have enough food," Mom explained. "And here is how you can both help."

Aaron and Nicki listened carefully. Mom said, "Let's get your red wagon. You can pull it along the sidewalk. When our neighbors bring their cans of soup, you can put the cans in the wagon."

Aaron and Nicki grinned. "That will be fun," Nicki said.

Soon Mom, Aaron and Nicki were pulling their wagon along the sidewalk. They stopped at each neighbor's house. Some neighbors gave cans of tomato soup. Some gave vegetable soup. Some gave cans of Nicki's favorite kind—chicken noodle!

"This wagon is getting HEAVY!" Aaron said.

"I'll help you the rest of the way," Nicki said. Together they pulled the wagon to their house.

"Look at all the cans of soup!" Mom said. "We have enough soup for lots of boys and girls."

Aaron and Nicki helped Mom move the cans from the wagon to a box in the car. "Wait!" said Nicki. "WE forgot to give soup!"

"You're right," Mom said. "Get the kind of soup from the cupboard you think the children will like."

Aaron and Nicki got several cans and put them in the box.

"Now we'll take all these cans of soup to the food bank. That's where the boys' and girls' parents can get them," Mom said. Aaron and Nicki were glad they could help to share all that tasty soup. "I think the boys and girls will like the chicken noodle soup best!" Nicki said.

Let's Talk About the Story

What did Aaron and Nicki have for lunch? What kind did Nicki like best? What did they decide to do? Why did Aaron's wagon become hard to pull? How were Aaron and Nicki kind?

Our Bible says, "Be kind to the poor and you will be happy." Let's say this Bible verse together. Repeat Bible verse with children. **Let's thank God for the good things we have and ask Him to help us be kind to others.** Pray briefly.

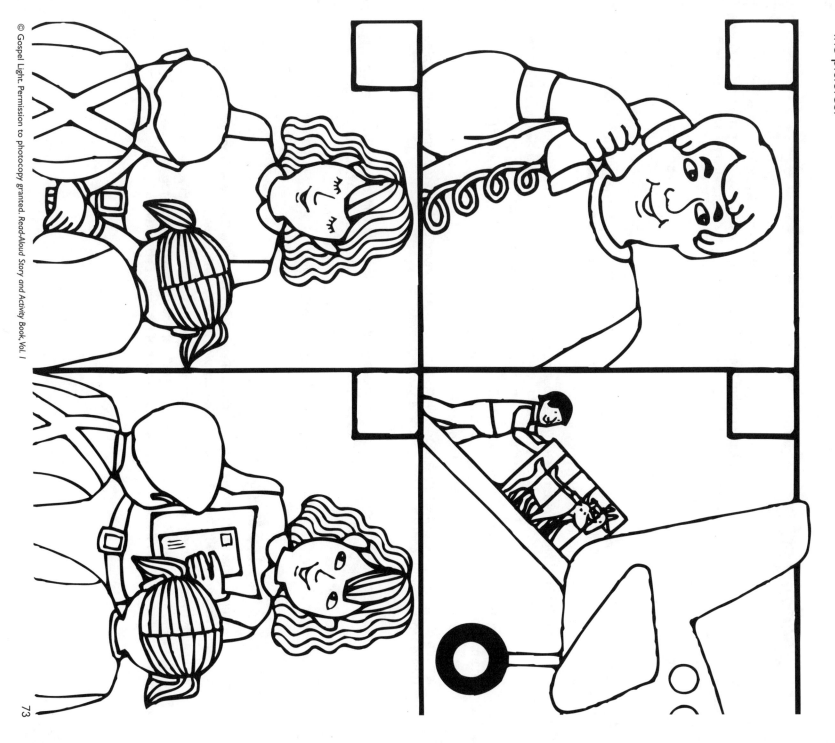

"Tell the good news about Jesus." (See Acts 8:35.)

Write a 1 in the picture box that shows what happened first. Write a 2 in the picture box that shows what happened second. Write a 3 in the picture box that shows what happened third. Write a 4 in the picture box that shows what happened last. (Younger children may point to the pictures.) Color the pictures.

Read-Aloud Story and Activity

1. Make a copy of Story Picture 34 for yourself and each child. Gather materials; color and complete your copy.

2. **Listen to find out what is in the letter this lady is holding.** Read story and show completed Story Picture 34.

3. Distribute materials. Use Let's Talk About the Story ideas as children complete pictures.

The Special Letter

"We have a special surprise today," said Mrs. Dodd, Colin's Sunday School teacher. All the children watched as she took a letter out of its envelope. "This letter is from Mr. Jiminez, our missionary in South America. Mr. Jiminez teaches in a school where boys and girls learn that Jesus loves them." Mrs. Dodd unfolded the letter and read:

Dear Kindergarten Boys and Girls:

Many children here in our school do not have enough milk to drink. Could you send powdered milk for them? Please pray that many people will help. The children here in our school love Jesus, just like you do.

Your friend, Mr. Jiminez

After Mrs. Dodd read the letter, everyone was quiet. They thought about Mr. Jiminez and the children in his school. Then they prayed that God would help the children to have the milk they needed.

"Why did Mr. Jiminez ask us to send POWDERED milk?" asked Colin.

"South America is a long way from here. Milk in bottles or cartons would spoil by the time it got to South America," Mrs. Dodd explained. "Mr. Jiminez can mix water with powdered milk and it will be like our milk," Mrs. Dodd continued. "Each Sunday let's bring some of our money to buy powdered milk."

On the way home from Sunday School, Colin told Mom and Dad about Mr. Jiminez's letter. "I wish we could send them a cow," Colin said. "Then they'd have lots of milk!"

"That gives me an idea," Dad said as he drove into the driveway.

As soon as they came into the house, Dad called someone on the phone and talked a long time. When he was finished, he called, "Colin! Mom! I've got some exciting news!"

Mom and Colin hurried to hear Dad's news.

"I've been talking to Mr. Ortega," Dad said. "He raises goats on his farm. When I told him about the children needing milk, he said he would send two goats to Mr. Jiminez in South America." Colin and Mom laughed!

"How wonderful!" Mom said. "Now the children will have PLENTY of milk to drink!"

"We asked God to help the children have milk," Colin said. "And He did!"

Let's Talk About the Story

What did Mr. Jiminez ask in his letter? How did the children help? What did Colin wish they could send to Mr. Jiminez? What was Dad's news? How did God answer the children's prayer?

The children were helping Mr.Jiminez so that he could tell the children in South America more about Jesus. Our Bible says, "Tell the good news about Jesus." **Let's say this Bible verse together.** Repeat Bible verse with children. **We can thank God for the good news of His love. Let's pray!** Pray briefly.

"God's love for us is great." (See 1 John 3:1.)

Draw a circle around the pictures of great things the Lord has done. Connect the dots. Color the picture.

Story Picture 35

Read-Aloud Story and Activity

1. Make a copy of Story Picture 35 for yourself and each child. Gather materials; color and complete your copy.

2. **Listen to find out what these children are praying about.** Read story and show completed Story Picture 35.

3. Distribute materials. Use Let's Talk About the Story ideas as children complete pictures.

Thanking God

"Jill, Ryan!" Mom called. "Please come here."

Ryan and Jill ran into the house. Mom was sitting in the living room. She looked worried. "What's the matter?" Ryan asked.

"Your grandma is very sick. She has to go to the hospital," Mom said. "Grandpa is coming to stay with us until she is well."

Jill sat down by Mom. "I'm glad Grandpa is going to stay with us," Jill said. She was quiet for a minute. Then she asked, "How can we help Grandma?"

"We can pray and ask God to make her well," Mom answered.

Every night when the children prayed, they asked God to take care of Grandma and make her well again.

Two days went by and then three. Then it was time to go to Sunday School. Ryan told his teacher, "My grandpa is staying with us because my grandma is sick in the hospital."

"We'll pray for your grandma," said Mrs. Lee, Ryan's teacher. Later in the morning she said, "Boys and girls, Jill and Ryan's grandma is sick in the hospital. Let's ask God to help her."

The children prayed. They thanked God for the doctors and nurses and asked God to help Jill and Ryan's grandma.

That afternoon, Ryan and Jill showed their grandpa some pictures they made. "When you visit Grandma today," Ryan said, "will you give these to her? We made them in Sunday School. Tell her we all prayed for her."

"Thank you," said Grandpa. "Grandma will be glad to know you are praying for her."

Every day Grandpa went to the hospital to see Grandma. Often Daddy or Mommy went with him. Then one day Grandpa and Daddy came home from the hospital with happy smiles. "Grandma is getting well and will be coming home in a few days," Daddy said.

Jill and Ryan could hardly wait to go to Sunday School to tell the good news! The next day, they hurried to the kindergarten room. "Mrs. Lee," Jill shouted. "God helped my grandma. She's getting well. And she's coming home soon!"

Later Mrs. Lee told all the children the good news, and all the children prayed, "Thank You, God, for helping Jill and Ryan's grandma be well."

Let's Talk About the Story

Why did Grandpa come to stay at Jill and Ryan's house? How did Jill and Ryan help Grandma? How did the children at Sunday School help? When Grandma was better, what did the children do?

God shows His love for us in many ways! Our Bible says, "God's love for us is great." Let's say this Bible verse together. Repeat Bible verse with children. **We can thank God for the ways He shows His love. Let's pray!** Pray briefly.

FOLD

"In God I trust; I will not be afraid." Psalm 56:4

Connect the broken lines. Fold flap back on dotted line.
Unfold flap to show what Marta found. Color the picture.

Story Picture 36

Read-Aloud Story and Activity

1. Make a copy of Story Picture 36 for yourself and each child. Gather materials; color and complete your copy.

2. **Listen to find out why this girl looks unhappy.** Read story and show completed Story Picture 36.

3. Distribute materials. Use Let's Talk About the Story ideas as children complete pictures.

The Great Big Dog

Today was Marta's first day at kindergarten. She and Mom were walking to school. They heard a loud "Woof-woof-woof!" And then they saw a big dog behind a fence.

Marta was afraid. She grabbed her mom and began to cry. "Maybe the dog didn't like our walking by the fence," said Mom as she dried Marta's tears. "Now let's go on to school."

Mrs. Lee was Marta's teacher. She smiled. Marta smiled, too, and said good-bye to her mom. Soon she forgot about the big dog—until it was time to go home.

"Ready to go?" smiled Marta's big brother, Juan.

"Oh, Juan, do we have to walk past that big dog?" asked Marta. She told Juan about the big dog. And she felt ready to cry again!

"That dog won't hurt you!" Juan said.

Just as they came to the fence, the big dog barked, "Woof-woof-woof!" Juan and Marta ran past as fast as they could!

Every day on the way to school Mom walked Marta past the barking dog. Every afternoon on the way home, Juan took Marta's hand when the dog barked.

But one day after school, Juan didn't come for Marta. Mrs. Lee explained, "Juan had to go home early today."

"I'm going to stop being afraid of the big dog," Marta said. "Good-bye, Mrs. Lee." And Marta started walking home all by herself.

When she got near the fence where the big dog lived, she began to be afraid. But she stopped before she got there. She prayed, *Dear God, please help me not to be afraid. In Jesus' name, amen.* Then she thought, *If I'm really not afraid, I'll walk instead of run past the dog.*

"Woof-woof-woof!" barked the big dog. But Marta didn't run! She just kept walking with her eyes straight ahead. Then she heard a tiny "yip-yip-yip" beside her feet. She looked down and there was a little puppy. Marta picked up the puppy and looked over the fence. She saw lots of puppies. And the big dog was playing with them. Then a man came out of the house. "Is this your puppy?" Marta asked him.

"Yes, thank you for bringing him back," said the man as he walked over to the fence and took the puppy from Marta.

"Is that big dog their mother?" Marta wanted to know.

"Yes, she is the best mother you ever saw," the man said. The big dog came over to the fence. "Would you like to pet her?" the man asked.

Marta reached through the fence and petted the mother dog's head. "I won't be afraid of the big dog anymore," Marta said as she walked home.

Let's Talk About the Story

Why was Marta afraid? What did Marta do that helped her when she was afraid? What noise did she hear at her feet? What made the noise? Why do you think the big dog barked?

Even when we're afraid, God loves us and helps us. Our Bible says, "In God I trust; I will not be afraid." Let's say this Bible verse together. Repeat Bible verse with children. **Let's thank God for His love and help, even when we're afraid.** Pray briefly.

"God will help you." 1 Chronicles 12:18

God helps us to have food.
On the blanket, draw the food you like to eat at a picnic.
Draw bread for the squirrels. Color the picture.

Read-Aloud Story and Activity

1. Make a copy of Story Picture 37 for yourself and each child. Gather materials; color and complete your copy.

2. **Listen to find out what this girl is doing.** Read story and show completed Story Picture 37.

3. Distribute materials. Use Let's Talk About the Story ideas as children complete pictures.

Surprises for Jennifer

Mommy, Aunt Peg and Jennifer were going for a walk in the woods.

"A picnic, a picnic," sang Jennifer. "We're going on a picnic!"

"'Take your sweater," said Mommy. "The breeze will be cool in the woods."

"What's in the picnic basket?" asked Aunt Peg.

"Sandwiches and carrots and apples," said Mommy. "And I have a surprise in the thermos."

"I have a surprise, too," smiled Aunt Peg.

"What is it? What is it?" asked Jennifer.

"Wait and see," answered Aunt Peg.

"Will I like to eat it?" asked Jennifer.

Aunt Peg laughed. "No, I don't think so, Jennifer. It is somebody else's picnic." Jennifer wondered whose picnic Aunt Peg was talking about!

Jennifer liked to walk with Mommy and Aunt Peg in the woods. The new green leaves on the trees waved in the breeze and chipmunks and squirrels were hopping high in the trees.

Soon Mommy and Aunt Peg and Jennifer came to a place where they put a blanket on the ground. They opened the picnic basket. Aunt Peg put the paper bag she was carrying by the picnic basket.

Jennifer sat on a log. She munched loudly on a carrot while she held her sandwich on her lap. "What's the surprise in the thermos?" she asked.

Mommy smiled and opened the thermos. "It's hot chocolate," she said.

Jennifer sipped some good hot chocolate from the cup Mommy handed here. "I like this surprise," she said. "Aunt Peg, what is your surprise?"

Aunt Peg opened her bag. She emptied it on the ground. All that was in the bag were pieces of dry bread!

"Watch carefully," Aunt Peg said. They sat very quietly and watched.

Suddenly a squirrel came—swish, hop, swish—right down the side of the tree. Another squirrel, then another, ran whoosh down the trees to get the bread!

Jennifer smiled, "God helped us have a good picnic, and I think we helped the squirrels have a good picnic, too!"

Let's Talk About the Story

Why did Mommy and Aunt Peg and Jennifer go to the woods? What did they eat for their picnic lunch? What was Mommy's surprise? Aunt Peg's?

God loves and helps us. Our Bible says, "God will help you." Let's say this Bible verse together. Repeat Bible verse with children. **Let's tell God we are glad He loves and helps us.** Pray briefly.

STOP

Willow Street

ONE WAY

START

Cut.

FOLD

"God is with you wherever you go." (See Joshua 1:9.)

Cut out the car puppet. Fold and tape ends together to fit finger. Move car along to find Willow Street. Color the road to find the puppies.

Story Picture 38

Read-Aloud Story and Activity

1. Make a copy of Story Picture 38 for yourself and each child. Gather materials; color and complete your copy.

2. **Listen to find out where this car is going.** Read story and show completed Story Picture 38.

3. Distribute materials. Use Let's Talk About the Story ideas as children complete pictures.

A Puppy for Andrew

"Justin! Ansley!" called Andrew as he came running out of his house to Justin and Ansley's back porch. He knocked at the door. "I'm going to get a PUPPY today!" Andrew shouted as Justin opened the door. "Dad said you and Ansley can come with me to get my puppy."

"Goody! Goody!" shouted Ansley and Justin. They asked their Mom—to make sure it was OK to go—and then they ran out with Andrew to his dad's car.

"Where are the puppies?" Andrew wanted to know as they rode along.

Andrew's dad was looking carefully at the street signs. "The puppies are at a house on Willow Street," he answered. Andrew's dad turned the corner and drove down another road. "I think Willow Street is this way," he said.

But they drove and drove. Still they didn't get to Willow Street. They passed many houses and stores. At last Andrew's dad stopped the car at the side of the road. "I was sure Willow Street was this way," he said. "Let me see if I can find Willow Street on the map."

"Are we lost, Dad?" Andrew asked.

"I don't like to be lost," said Justin.

Ansley looked at Justin and Andrew. Then she looked at Andrew's dad. Ansley didn't like to be lost either.

"We're not really lost," Andrew's dad said. "We just haven't found Willow Street yet." Andrew's dad turned the car around and started back down the road. He smiled at the three children. "I'm glad God takes care of us wherever we go, aren't you? God is always with us, even when we can't find the right street."

Justin and Ansley and Andrew nodded their heads. Of course God was taking care of them! All of a sudden, Andrew's dad saw something. He stopped the car. "There's a sign on the ground," he said. "The wind must have blown it down."

"What does the sign say?" Andrew asked.

"Willow Street!" Andrew's dad said in surprise. He drove the car down Willow Street.

Soon they were inside a house looking at five fat puppies. Two were brown. Two puppies were black. And one puppy was the color of butter.

"Let's take the one that looks like butter," Andrew said.

"All right. We'll take that yellow one that looks like a butterball," Andrew's dad said.

"Butterball!" Andrew laughed as the puppy licked his finger. "That's a good name for my puppy!"

Let's Talk About the Story

Where did Ansley and Justin go with Andrew and his dad? Did Ansley and Justin and Andrew think they were lost? Why couldn't they find Willow Street? What did Andrew's dad help them remember?

Wherever we go, God is with us. Our Bible says, "God is with you wherever you go." Let's say this Bible verse together. Repeat Bible verse with children. **Let's thank God that He is with us and loves us wherever we go.** Pray briefly.

"Jesus said, 'Love each other as I have loved you.'" (See John 15:12.)

Fold flap forward on dotted line. Put an ✗ on the places Whitney and her family looked for her shoe.
Open the flap to see who found her shoe. Color the picture.

FOLD

Story Picture 39

Read-Aloud Story and Activity

1. Make a copy of Story Picture 39 for yourself and each child. Gather materials; color and complete your copy.

2. **Listen to find out where this girl found her shoe.** Read story and show completed Story Picture 39.

3. Distribute materials. Use Let's Talk About the Story ideas as children complete pictures.

The Lost Shoe

"I can't find my shoe," Whitney called to her mom. Whitney was hurrying to get dressed, so she could go outside to play.

"Look in your closet," Mom called. Whitney looked in her closet for her shoe. "It's not there," Whitney called back.

"I'll help you look," Mom said as she came into Whitney's bedroom. Mom looked under the bed. But Whitney's shoe was not there. Whitney looked under the chair. But her shoe was not there either.

"Maybe you took it off in the living room," Mom said. So Whitney and Mom went to look for the shoe in the living room. Whitney got down on the floor and looked under the couch.

"What are you looking for?" Daddy asked Whitney and Mom.

"We're looking for Whitney's shoe," Mom answered. "Have you seen it?"

"No," Daddy said, "but I'll help you look for it."

Under the piano and on the chairs, in the corners and up on the shelf—Mom and Daddy and Whitney looked for Whitney's shoe. Then Whitney's brother Joshua came into the room. "What are you looking for?" he asked.

"We're looking for my shoe," Whitney answered. So Joshua began to look, too—under the table and under the chairs, behind the door and beside the fireplace.

At last Daddy said. "I wonder where that shoe could possibly be!"

"Do you suppose Whitney's shoe could be outside?" Mom asked.

Joshua started to run outside to look for the lost shoe. As he went through the kitchen to the back door, he saw their big dog, Pal, with something in her mouth. Joshua looked closer. Then he shouted, "Look! Pal found Whitney's shoe!"

Mom and Daddy and Whitney hurried into the kitchen. And sure enough. Pal was holding the shoe in her mouth. Whitney took the shoe from Pal.

"Woof, woof, woof!" barked Pal. She wagged her tail back and forth.

Daddy laughed. "Pal is trying to tell you she helped look for your shoe, too."

"Everybody helped me," Whitney said, "even Pal!" And Whitney patted Pal's head. "Thank you, Pal, for finding my shoe."

Let's Talk About the Story

What did Whitney lose? Who helped Whitney look for her shoe? Where did the family look for Whitney's shoe? Who found her shoe? How do you think Whitney's shoe got in the kitchen?

Whitney's family all showed love when they helped her. God loves us, too. That helps us show love to other people. Our Bible says, "Jesus said, 'Love each other as I have loved you.' " Let's say this Bible verse together. Repeat Bible verse with children. **We can thank God for the ways He shows His love. Let's pray!** Pray briefly.

"Let us love one another." 1 John 4:7

Helping each other is a way to show love. Color the picture. Cut out paintbrush. Use paper fastener to attach brush to Craig's hand. Show how Craig helped.

Attach brush here.

Cut.

Story Picture 40

Read-Aloud Story and Activity

1. Make a copy of Story Picture 40 for yourself and each child. Gather materials; color and complete your copy.

2. **Listen to find out what this boy is doing.** Read story and show completed Story Picture 40.

3. Distribute materials. Use Let's Talk About the Story ideas as children complete pictures.

The Help-Daddy Shirt

Craig was a good helper at home. There were lots of things he did without being told, like dressing himself and coming straight home from kindergarten. There were some things Craig liked best to do, like mixing the meatballs for Mom. He ESPECIALLY liked helping his daddy.

One day when Craig came home from school, Daddy was lying on his back on the lawn. There were paint cans and brushes all around him. "What are you doing, Daddy?" Craig asked. "Are you sick?"

"I've been painting this fence all afternoon, and my back hurts from bending over," Daddy answered.

"Let me help you, Daddy!" begged Craig. "I can paint the low parts, so you don't have to bend over."

"Do you have on old clothes?" Daddy asked.

"I got this shirt a long time ago," Craig answered.

"Okay," Daddy said. "Maybe you can paint this corner down here for me. My hand is too big."

Quickly Craig bent down to look at the corner of the fence. "I can do it, Daddy!" he said.

"Good!" Daddy said. Daddy gave Craig a paintbrush and showed him how to dip it in the paint just right. Craig bent down again and brushed the paint on the fence back and forth, back and forth, just like Daddy showed him. Soon Craig's corner was all finished.

"Look, Daddy," Craig said. As Daddy turned to look, he bumped the paint can and it started to slip off the fence. Craig jumped up and caught it. A little paint splashed out on Craig's shirt.

"Whew!" Daddy said and laughed. "Thanks a lot! I don't know what I'd do without my helper!"

"Am I a good helper?" asked Craig.

"You sure are!" Daddy said. "Now see if you can reach down and paint this corner and that one," Daddy pointed.

Painting the corners was easy for Craig. Soon he was done.

"I guess we'd better get cleaned up for dinner," Daddy said. Just then, Mommy came out the kitchen door. "Craig! What happened?"

"I was helping Daddy paint the fence," Craig said.

Daddy laughed as he looked at their paint-spattered clothes. "Craig painted the corners I couldn't reach. And he caught the paint can, so it didn't spill all over the lawn. I guess good helpers get messy!"

"I like to help Daddy paint!" said Craig.

Mommy laughed. "We can call that shirt your 'help-daddy' shirt."

"That's a good idea," Daddy said. "Now, Craig, let's go get cleaned up!"

Craig smiled as he looked down at his help-daddy shirt. "Daddy," Craig asked, "when can I help you again?"

Let's Talk About the Story

How did Craig help Daddy? How did Craig's shirt get paint on it? What did Mommy call Craig's shirt?

God made the people in our families. He wants us to love each other. Our Bible says, "Let us love one another." Let's say this Bible verse together. Repeat Bible verse with children. **We can ask God to help us show love to the people in our families.** Pray briefly.

"Always try to be kind." 1 Thessalonians 5:15
Fold paper forward on line. Show Scene 1; then show Scene 2.
Find 12 eggs hidden in the picture. Color the picture.

SCENE 1

SCENE 2

FOLD

Story Picture 41

Read-Aloud Story and Activity

1. Make a copy of Story Picture 41 for yourself and each child. Gather materials; color and complete your copy.

2. **Listen to find out what these children are looking for.** Read story and show completed Story Picture 41.

3. Distribute materials. Use Let's Talk About the Story ideas as children complete pictures.

One More Egg

Molly and Nathaniel were visiting Grandma and Grandpa's farm. What fun it was to help Grandma gather eggs!

"1,2,3,4,5,6,7,8,9,10,11," Grandma said as she counted the eggs. "We need just one more egg! Then we'll have a full carton to give to the Martin family."

"Why do you give eggs to the Martin family?" Molly wanted to know.

"The Martins have a big family," Grandma said. "And we have more eggs than we need. I like to help by sharing our eggs with them each week."

Molly and Nathaniel followed Grandma into the kitchen. She opened the refrigerator and put the eggs inside.

Then Nathaniel said, "Maybe if we look again we can find one more egg." So he and Molly when out to the barnyard and looked in the manger where Grandpa put the hay for the horses. No egg. Molly went into the chicken house and looked in each nest again. No egg. Then Molly saw a little nest behind the door. And inside was an egg! Carefully she picked it up just the way Grandma had shown her. Then she ran to find Nathaniel.

"Look! Look! I found an egg!" Molly called. "Now we will have a full carton to give to the Martins."

Nathaniel came running, too. "Just wait till you see what I found behind the haystack! A big nest just full of eggs!" Nathaniel shouted. "Let's go tell Grandma."

Nathaniel and Molly ran to the house to share the big news.

"Grandma" Nathaniel called, "come see what I found!"

When Grandma saw the nest full of eggs, she laughed. "So this is where our setting hen has been hiding her eggs!"

"Can we give these eggs to the Martin family, too?" Nathaniel wanted to know.

"No," Grandma answered. "Some eggs must hatch into little chicks, so they can grow to be chickens and lay more eggs. Let's watch! This egg is ready to hatch! See the little hole in the shell? The chick is pecking its way out."

As Molly and Nathaniel and Grandma watched, an egg began to crack open. Out wobbled a tiny, wet baby chick.

Molly and Nathaniel looked at the little wet chick. "Can we hold the baby chick?" Molly asked.

"No," Grandma answered. "It needs its mother to keep it warm. We'd better go now, so she'll come back to her nest."

The next day Molly and Nathaniel counted nine yellow chicks.

"Little chicks, when you grow up," Molly said, "you can lay lots of eggs for us—and for the Martin family."

Let's Talk About the Story

Why did Grandma need one more egg? Where did Molly find another egg? What did Nathaniel find? What happened as Molly and Nathaniel and Grandma watched the eggs? What did Molly tell the baby chicks?

God wants us to show our love by being kind to others. Our Bible says, "Always try to be kind." Let's say this Bible verse together. Repeat Bible verse with children. **We can ask God to help us be kind to our friends.** Pray briefly.

"Speak the truth to each other." Zechariah 8:16

Color the picture. Draw stripes on the ball.

Story Picture 42

Read-Aloud Story and Activity

1. Make a copy of Story Picture 42 for yourself and each child. Gather materials; color and complete your copy.

2. **Listen to find out what happened to this girl.** Read story and show completed Story Picture 42.

3. Distribute materials. Use Let's Talk About the Story ideas as children complete pictures.

Monique's New Ball

One of the birthday presents Monique liked best was a big ball with blue and yellow stripes around it. After everyone had gone home from her birthday party, Monique's Aunt Winnie told her, "We have one rule about playing with your new ball. You must not bounce it in the house. Bounce it out in the backyard."

"I won't bounce it in the house," Monique said.

Monique was busy all the next morning playing with her birthday presents—a new doll with doll clothes in a little pink suitcase, a box of crayons and lots of paper and two new puzzles.

After lunch, Monique remembered her pretty ball with the blue and yellow stripes. But she forgot her aunt's rule. Monique gave her ball a little bounce against the door in the living room. And Prince, her dog, ran after it. "That was fun, Prince," Monique said. "Let's do it again." Monique laughed as Prince tried to put the ball in his mouth. The ball was just too big for Prince. Monique bounced and bounced the ball against the door. And each time, Prince ran after it.

But one time, Monique's ball did not bounce against the door. The ball hit the lamp table. Crash! The lamp fell off the table and onto the floor. Quickly Monique went to pick up the lamp.

Aunt Winnie heard the crash and came running into the living room. "Are you OK?" she asked Monique.

"I'm OK," Monique answered.

"What happened?" Aunt Winnie wanted to know.

Monique looked at Prince. She thought, *I could say that Prince knocked off the lamp.* But she knew she should tell the truth. "Um . . . my ball hit the lamp," she said.

"I'm glad you told me the truth," Aunt Winnie said. "But what about our rule?" Monique then remembered Aunt Winnie's rule: do not bounce the ball in the house. Monique was very quiet.

Then she whispered, "I'll remember next time. So will Prince."

"NEXT time both of you will play ball outside," Aunt Winnie said. She gave Monique a hug and Prince a pat on the head.

Let's Talk About the Story

What gifts did Monique get for her birthday? What color was her ball? What was her aunt's rule about bouncing the ball? What did Monique forget? Then what happened? What did Monique tell her aunt?

God wants us to show love in our families by telling the truth. Our Bible says, "Speak the truth to each other." Let's say this Bible verse together. Repeat Bible verse with children. **Let's thank God for our families. We'll ask Him to help us tell the truth at home.** Pray briefly.

"Forgive each other." (See Colossians 3:13.)

Connect the dots. Color the picture.

Story Picture 43

Read-Aloud Story and Activity

1. Make a copy of Story Picture 43 for yourself and each child. Gather materials; color and complete your copy.

2. **Listen to find out what this boy is saying.** Read story and show completed Story Picture 43.

3. Distribute materials. Use Let's Talk About the Story ideas as children complete pictures.

Austin's Pool

"When's Mommy coming home from work?" Austin asked his grandma.

"It won't be much longer," Grandma answered.

"But it's already been a long time," Austin said sadly as he stood looking out the front window.

Today Austin's mom was bringing home a wading pool. Austin already had on his swimsuit! When Austin heard his mom's car turn in the driveway, he RAN outside.

"Did you bring the wading pool?" he shouted as he ran.

Mom laughed. "It's right here." She lifted a big box from the car's trunk and carried it to the backyard.

Soon Mom and Grandma had the wading pool ready to fill with water. Austin turned the water faucet handle as hard as he could. Soon the pool was full of cool water!

Austin stepped in, one foot at a time. Oooooh! The cool water felt good! Austin had fun playing with his boats while Mom and Grandma watched.

Then his big brother, Michael, called from the door, "Austin, can I play in your pool?"

"Yes!" Austin answered.

Soon Michael was in the pool. For a while, both boys had fun playing in the wading pool.

Then Michael said, "Look, Austin." As Austin looked up, Michael splashed lots of water in his face. It scared Austin! Some of the water got up his nose. It stung his eyes. Austin felt like crying. Michael just laughed and splashed Austin again. Austin wanted to hit Michael or splash Michael back, really hard!

But Austin looked over at his mom. She looked at Austin in a way that helped him remember what she said about using words.

"Michael, I don't LIKE it when you splash me!" Austin said. "Please don't do it anymore!"

Michael stopped splashing. He looked down at the boats in the pool. "I'm sorry," Michael said. "I didn't know you don't like to get splashed. My friend Drew splashes me all the time!"

"Well, I don't like it!" Austin said as he rubbed the water out of his eyes. After a minute, Austin said, "I know. Let's race the boats. The blue boat can be yours. And the red boat is mine."

"OK," Michael answered. He picked up the blue boat. "Ready! Set! Go!"

Let's Talk About the Story

What did Austin's mom bring home? What did Michael do? Why do you think Austin didn't like getting splashed? What did Austin tell Michael? Then what did Michael do? Which boat do you think won the race?

God wants us to forgive the people in our families. Our Bible says, "Forgive each other." Let's say this Bible verse together. Repeat Bible verse with children. **We can ask God to help us forgive the people we live with.** Pray briefly.

"Love the Lord your God." Matthew 22:37

Draw the snack on the table. Color the picture.

Story Picture 44

Read-Aloud Story and Activity

1. Make a copy of Story Picture 44 for yourself and each child. Gather materials; color and complete your copy.

2. **Listen to find out what story these people are reading**. Read story and show completed Story Picture 44.

3. Distribute materials. Use Let's Talk About the Story ideas as children complete pictures.

Andrea's Friend

"Mom, does Mrs. Garcia have any children?" Andrea asked.

"Yes," Mom answered, "but they have all grown up and moved far away. I'm sure she is lonesome for them." Andrea was sorry Mrs. Garcia was lonesome. Mrs. Garcia lived next door. She always smiled and waved to Andrea and her mom.

On the Monday after Andrea came home from kindergarten, she asked, "Mom, may I go over to Mrs. Garcia's house? I have something I want to show her."

"Yes," Mom answered, "but don't stay too long."

Andrea ran up the steps to Mrs. Garcia's front door and rang the doorbell. Mrs. Garcia was surprised to see Andrea. "Why, hello, Andrea. Please come in," she said.

"Hello, Mrs. Garcia," said Andrea. "Mom said I could come to visit you. I have something to show you."

They went into the living room and sat down together on the big couch. "I brought my new Bible storybook," Andrea said. "It has pictures and stories in it. Do you want me to tell you about them?"

"Oh, yes," Mrs. Garcia answered. "I'd like to know about your Bible storybook."

"Here is the story we heard at Sunday School yesterday. This is Daniel," said Andrea. "These are his friends. They were very brave."

Then Andrea said, "That's the end." And she closed the Bible storybook.

"Let's have cookies and a glass of milk before you go," Mrs. Garcia suggested.

After they finished their snack, Andrea said, "I have to go home now. Thank you for the milk and cookies."

"Thank you for coming and sharing your Bible storybook with me," said Mrs. Garcia. "I hope you'll come again."

Andrea visited Mrs. Garcia many times after that. Each time she took her Bible storybook with her. And each time, she and Mrs. Garcia had a snack!

Let's Talk About the Story

Who did Andrea go to see? What did she take with her? What did she do with her Bible storybook? What did she and Mrs. Garcia have to eat? Why do you think Andrea went to visit Mrs. Garcia?

God wants us to do what is right. It is a way to show we love Him. Our Bible says, "Love the Lord your God." Let's say this Bible verse together. Repeat Bible verse with children. **Let's pray. We can thank God for helping us learn to love and obey Him.** Pray briefly.

"I trust in the Lord." Psalm 31:6

Connect the dots. Color the picture.

Story Picture 45

Read-Aloud Story and Activity

1. Make a copy of Story Picture 45 for yourself and each child. Gather materials; color and complete your copy.

2. **Listen to find out where these people are going.** Read story and show completed Story Picture 45.

3. Distribute materials. Use Let's Talk About the Story ideas as children complete pictures.

A Ride in the Rain

Daddy, Seth and Molly were taking Mom to the airport, so she could fly to a faraway city.

"I hear airplanes," Seth said. "We're near the airport!"

"I don't see any airplanes," Molly said.

"It's raining so hard, we can't SEE the airplanes," Daddy said. He slowly drove the car along the road.

"How can the pilot see where to fly the airplane in the rain?" Seth wanted to know.

"The pilot has special instruments that help him know EXACTLY where he is, even when he cannot see," Mom said.

Daddy stopped the car beside a big building. Before Mom got out, she kissed Seth and Molly and Daddy. "I'll be home next Saturday," Mom said. "See you then."

"Bye, Mom," Seth and Molly said as they hugged her.

"We'll all be here to meet you," Daddy said. As Mom opened the car door to get out, Seth and Molly could feel the rain blowing in. Mom closed the car door quickly and ran toward the big building.

Daddy started the car. Swish, swish, swish went the windshield wipers as Daddy drove the car away from the airport.

"I wish Mom didn't have to go when it's raining," Molly said sadly.

"Will Mom be all right?" Seth asked.

"We have someone who knows about Mom's trip on the airplane," Daddy said, "someone who loves and cares about Mom very much. Can you think who that might be?"

"It's God, that's who!" Seth said.

"Yes," Daddy said. "God cares for each one of us. We can trust Him to take care of Mom and take care of us, too!"

"Even way up in an airplane?" Molly wanted to know.

"Yes, even when Mom is up in an airplane," Daddy answered. "'I trust in the Lord' is a Bible verse we can remember when we think about Mom up in the airplane."

"I'm glad God knows about Mom up in the airplane," Seth said.

Seth and Molly were quiet for a few minutes. Then Molly said, "Let's make our hands be windshield wipers, like the ones on our car." So all the way home Seth and Molly moved their hands back and forth, back and forth while the windshield wipers on the car went swish, swish, swish.

Let's Talk About the Story

Where did Seth and Molly and Daddy take Mom? Why couldn't they see the airplanes? Who did Daddy say was taking care of Mom? What Bible verse did Daddy remember?

God loves us. He always cares for us and helps us. Our Bible says, "I trust in the Lord." Let's say this Bible verse together. Repeat Bible verse with children. **Let's thank God that we can trust Him.** Pray briefly.

"We will listen and obey." Deuteronomy 5:27

Color the picture. Draw the missing parts in the picture. Draw stick figures to show what children should do when their mom calls them.

Read-Aloud Story and Activity

1. Make a copy of Story Picture 46 for yourself and each child. Gather materials; color and complete your copy.

2. **Listen to find out why this mom is calling her children.** Read story and show completed Story Picture 46.

3. Distribute materials. Use Let's Talk About the Story ideas as children complete pictures.

When Mom Called

"Christine! Philip! Christine! Philip!" Mom called and called. Christine and Philip were next door. They were digging tunnels in the sandbox in Ashley's backyard. They heard their mom calling.

"We have to go now," Christine said. "Mom's calling us. Come on, Philip."

"Wait. I want to drive my car through the tunnel more," Philip said.

"But Mom wants us. She's calling us," Christine said.

"I don't want to go yet," Philip answered.

"Christine! Philip! Christine! Philip!" Mom called and called. Christine and Philip did not answer.

After a while Philip took his little car out of the tunnel. "Let's go now," he said to Christine. She wiped sand off her hands. "Bye, Ashley," they said.

Slowly Christine and Philip walked into the house.

"Where have you been? I called and called you both," Mom said. "I was just about ready to go and find you!"

"Did you need us?" Christine asked.

"I needed you both right away," Mom answered. "I needed to help you get ready for a visit to the zoo."

"Oh! When?" Philip asked excitedly.

"Your Uncle Bill stopped to take you with him on some errands. He thought you might like to stop on the way back and see the new baby elephants at the zoo," Mom explained.

Christine jumped up and down. "Oh, goody, goody! When's he coming to get us?" she asked.

"Your Uncle Bill was already here." Mom said. "That's the reason I called and called you. He waited as long as he could. But he had to go without you."

Christine and Philip stopped smiling. They wished and wished they had not stayed to play in the sandbox at Ashley's house! A big tear slid down Christine's face. Philip wiped a teary eye with the back of his hand.

"Uncle Bill said he would take you another day," Mom said. Christine and Philip had to wait many, many days; but finally, Uncle Bill took them to the zoo. They saw the new baby elephants chasing each other and waving their trunks in the air.

"I wonder if baby elephants always come when their mother calls them?" Uncle Bill asked.

Christine and Philip wondered, too. Now they knew what THEY should do when their mom called!

Let's Talk About the Story

What did Christine and Philip do when their mom called them? Why didn't they answer their mom? What did Uncle Bill want them to do? What do you think Christine and Philip did the next time their mom called? What should you do when your mom or dad calls you?

God wants us to obey Him. It shows we love Him. Our Bible says, "We will listen and obey." Let's say this Bible verse together. Repeat Bible verse with children. **Let's pray. We can ask God for help when we don't want to obey.** Pray briefly.

"I pray to you, O Lord." Psalm 69:13

Thank You, God, for my family. Draw a ○ on each circle. Draw a □ on each square. Draw an ✗ in each triangle. Color the picture.

Read-Aloud Story and Activity

1. Make a copy of Story Picture 47 for yourself and each child. Gather materials; color and complete your copy.

2. **Listen to find out who helped this boy.** Read story and show completed Story Picture 47.

3. Distribute materials. Use Let's Talk About the Story ideas as children complete pictures.

Who Helped Colin?

"I'm going to ride my trike," Colin called as he ran outside. Colin climbed up on his tricycle and sat down on the red seat. He pressed his feet against the pedals. But nothing happened. His tricycle didn't MOVE! Colin pressed his foot down harder, but his tricycle still didn't move. Quickly Colin got off and ran into the house.

"Daddy, Daddy," Colin called. "My trike won't go."

"Well, let's see what's the trouble," Daddy said.

Colin and Daddy walked outside. Daddy looked at the trike wheels.

"Oh, I see," Daddy said. "One of the wheel spokes is bent. It's jammed against the frame."

"Can you fix it?" Colin asked.

"Yes," Daddy answered, "but I'll need to get my pliers from the garage."

While Daddy fixed the trike, Colin ran into the house to ask for something to eat.

"Well," Mommy said, "how about a glass of milk and some graham crackers?"

"Yummy," Colin said as he climbed onto his chair at the kitchen table.

Mommy got the carton of milk from the refrigerator. She poured the cold milk into Colin's glass. Then on a napkin she put three big graham crackers for Colin to eat.

"This tastes good. I'm hungry!" Colin said. He drank all his milk and ate every cracker—even the crumbs.

"Your trike's all fixed," Daddy said when he walked into the kitchen.

"Goody," Colin said. "'I'm ready to ride it." And out the door he ran. Soon Colin was zooming along on his tricycle.

That night when Colin was getting ready for bed, he and Daddy talked about the things Colin had done that day. "You fixed my trike, and I rode it for a long time," Colin remembered.

"And Mommy fixed your milk and crackers when you were hungry," Daddy said.

"We're glad to help you," Daddy said. "God is glad to help you, too."

Colin was quiet. Then in a soft voice Colin prayed, "Thank You, God, for my mommy and daddy. Thank You for helping me. In Jesus' name, amen."

Let's Talk About the Story

Why couldn't Colin ride his trike? Who fixed it? When Colin was hungry, who fixed his snack? While Colin was getting ready for bed, what did he do?

God helps us. Because we love Him, we can pray to Him. Our Bible says, "I pray to you, O Lord." Let's say this Bible verse together. Repeat Bible verse with children. **Let's pray right now! We can thank God for His help.** Pray briefly.

"Love is patient, love is kind." 1 Corinthians 13:4

Fold on line and show one scene at a time. Color the circles blue.
Color the triangles red. Color the squares yellow.

SCENE 1

FOLD

SCENE 2

Story Picture 48

Read-Aloud Story and Activity

1. Make a copy of Story Picture 48 for yourself and each child. Gather materials; color and complete your copy.

2. **Listen to find out what this girl is asking.** Read story and show completed Story Picture 48.

3. Distribute materials. Use Let's Talk About the Story ideas as children complete pictures.

Meg Is Patient

"Mom, would you read me a story, please?" Meg asked.

"When I have finished washing the dishes, I'll read to you," Mom answered.

Meg felt angry. She wanted Mom to read the story RIGHT NOW!

It seemed like a LONG time before Mom was through with the dishes. And just as she finished, there was a knock at the back door. It was their neighbor, Mrs. Cole. In one arm she held a bundle of red cloth. Beside her stood three-year-old Jonathan.

"Could you please help me sew the sleeve in this dress I am making? Mrs. Cole asked Meg's mom.

Meg opened her mouth. She was about to say, "NO, she can't. I want her to READ to me"! But Meg didn't say it. Her mom gave her a wink and then said to Mrs. Cole, "Why certainly! I'll be glad to help. Meg can play with Jonathan outside while we work on the dress."

Meg looked at her mom. She sighed. But she went outside with Jonathan and let him ride her trike while Meg played with the wagon. Then they played with Meg's big ball. Soon Mom and Mrs. Cole were finished. And Jonathan went home with his mother.

Meg went to her mom. "NOW can you read me a story?" she asked.

Mom looked at the clock. "Dad will be here soon, Meg. We need to get dinner started."

Meg looked at her mom and sighed again. She almost said, "But you PROMISED. Read NOW!" But she didn't. Instead, she went outside while her mother worked. She found some flowers in the yard and put them into a vase with water for the table.

As they ate dinner, Mom told Dad, "Meg was very patient today. She didn't whine or fuss because I couldn't read a story to her this afternoon. She played with Jonathan to help me and Mrs. Cole while we worked. She helped set the table for dinner. I think she should have a VERY long story time tonight! She knows how to be patient!"

"I'm glad to hear it!" said Dad. He reached over to hug Meg. "I'll be glad to read for an extra-long time tonight!"

Let's Talk About the Story

Why didn't Meg's mom read to her when Meg asked? What did Meg do to help? Why do you think it was hard for Meg to be patient?

God wants us to show we love Him. One way to do that is to be patient and kind. Our Bible says, "Love is patient, love is kind." Let's say this Bible verse together. Repeat Bible verse with children. **Let's pray and ask God to help us be kind and patient.** Pray briefly.

X

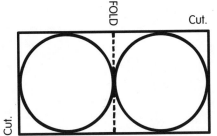

FOLD

Cut.

Cut.

"We will do everything the Lord has said." Exodus 19:8

Cut and fold ball. Tape one end of 3-inch (7.5 cm) string to X.
Tape other end to ball. Color the picture.

Story Picture 49

Read-Aloud Story and Activity

1. Make a copy of Story Picture 49 for yourself and each child. Gather materials; color and complete your copy.

2. **Listen to find out how Sophie obeyed.** Read story and show completed Story Picture 49.

3. Distribute materials. Use Let's Talk About the Story ideas as children complete pictures.

Sophie Makes a Friend

One afternoon Sophie came home from kindergarten frowning instead of smiling.

"My goodness, Sophie! What's the matter?" Mom asked.

"I don't like Amy!" Sophie said, still frowning.

"Let's have some graham crackers and talk about it," Mom said.

Mom and Sophie sat down at the kitchen table. Mom poured milk and put graham crackers on a plate. "Tell me what happened today," she said.

Sophie took a drink of milk. She chose a graham cracker from the plate. "Well," she began, "I was drawing a picture, and Amy made a big red mark on it with her crayon. She spoiled it."

Sophie finished eating her graham cracker. "It was a pretty picture," she said, "and I was going to write a story about it. I don't like Amy."

Mom took Sophie's hand. "I'm sorry Amy marked your picture," Mom said. "But, Sophie, the Bible tells us to love each other. That means loving Amy, even when she does something you don't like. That's hard to do! But God will help you if you ask Him."

Sophie thought about what Mom had said. That night when Sophie prayed, she asked God to help her love Amy.

The next day at school Sophie got a ball from the closet and began bouncing it. She saw Amy sitting on the bench. Sophie remembered what Mom had said.

"Amy," Sophie called, "want to play ball with me?"

Amy smiled. "OK!" she said.

First they bounced the ball back and forth. Then they sat down and rolled the ball to each other. Sophie and Amy had a good time playing together! Later they put the ball away and got jump ropes.

"How many times can you jump?" Amy asked.

The girls counted while Sophie jumped rope. "1, 2, 3, 4, 5 . . . 23, 24, 25." Sophie jumped 25 times before she missed. Then it was Amy's turn to jump.

Sophie counted, "1, 2, 3, 4, 5 . . . 23, 24, 25, 26, 27." Amy jumped the rope 27 times! "You're a good jumper," Sophie said.

Later when the children were back in the room, Mrs. Martin, their kindergarten teacher, said, "Amy, I'd like you to take this message to the office for me. You may choose a friend to go with you."

Amy looked at the children on the rug. "I choose Sophie," Amy said.

As Sophie and Amy walked to the office, Amy said, "I'm glad you're my friend, Sophie."

Sophie smiled. "I'm glad, too," she said.

Let's Talk About the Story

Why was Sophie frowning when she came home from school? What had Amy done? What did Sophie do about it? What did Sophie and Amy do together?

God wants us to obey Him and love others. Sometimes it is hard to obey. But our Bible says, "We will do everything the Lord has said." **Let's say this Bible verse together.** Repeat Bible verse with children. **We can ask God right now to help us obey Him and show His love.** Pray briefly.

"Teach me, O Lord." Psalm 119:33
Connect the dots. Draw candles on the birthday cake. Color the picture.

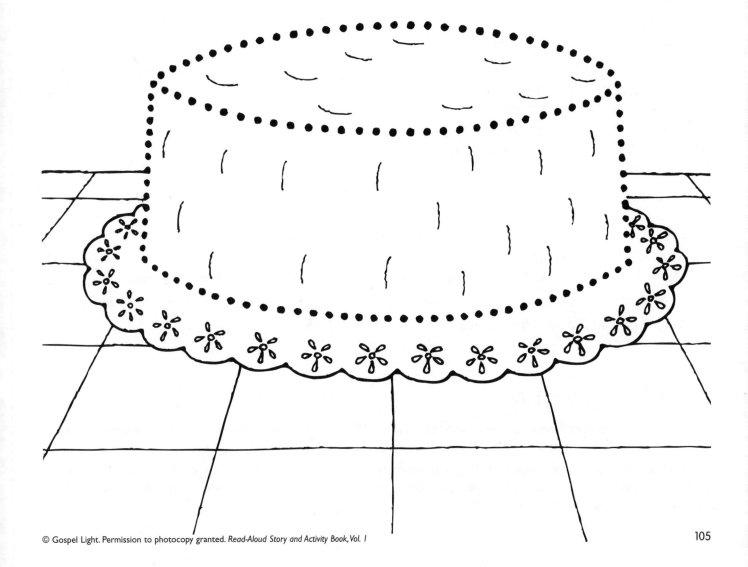

Read-Aloud Story and Activity

1. Make a copy of Story Picture 50 for yourself and each child. Gather materials; color and complete your copy.

2. **Listen to find out who this cake is for.** Read story and show completed Story Picture 50.

3. Distribute materials. Use Let's Talk About the Story ideas as children complete pictures

The Birthday Cake

After Daddy went to work one morning, Mommy said to Alex and Nicole, "Today is Daddy's birthday. Let's surprise him with a birthday cake."

"With candles?" Nicole wanted to know.

"Yes," Mommy answered. "With lots of candles!"

"Let's make chocolate frosting," Alex suggested

"That's a good idea," Mommy said. "Now let's get busy." Mommy got out the flour and salt and all the other things for the birthday cake.

"Let's play a game while we make the cake," Mommy said. "We'll do just what our poem says:

Sift the flour, beat the eggs,

Add some salt and a bit of nutmeg.

A spoon of butter, a cup of milk,

Stir and be as fine as silk.

What are you making, for goodness sake?

Shh! It's a secret! A birthday cake!"

Mommy and Alex and Nicole said the poem again and again. Soon Mommy poured the cake batter into the cake pans and put them in the oven.

After the cake was baked and cooled, Nicole and Alex watched Mommy pile frosting on the cake. Then she let Nicole and Alex stick pretty green candies on top of the cake.

"Can we lick the spoons?" Alex wanted to know.

"Of course!" Mommy said as she handed Alex and Nicole each a spoon. "That's part of the fun when we make a birthday cake."

After Alex and Nicole had eaten every bit of frosting out of the bowl, Mommy said, "Let's put our pretty tablecloth on the dining-room table."

Mommy and Alex spread the white tablecloth. Mommy put the cake in the middle of the table.

When it was time for Daddy to come home, Mommy and Nicole and Alex sat by the front window to wait for him.

"Daddy will be surprised when he sees his birthday cake!" Nicole said.

"I like birthdays," Alex said, "even when they're not mine!"

Let's Talk About the Story

What did Mommy and Alex and Nicole make? What did they put into the cake? What did Mommy let Alex and Nicole do? Why do you think they wanted to surprise Daddy?

**God teaches us to love others. But God will help us learn to do it. Our Bible says, "Teach me, O Lord."
Let's say this Bible verse together.** Repeat Bible verse with children. **We can ask God right now to teach us how to love people.** Pray briefly.

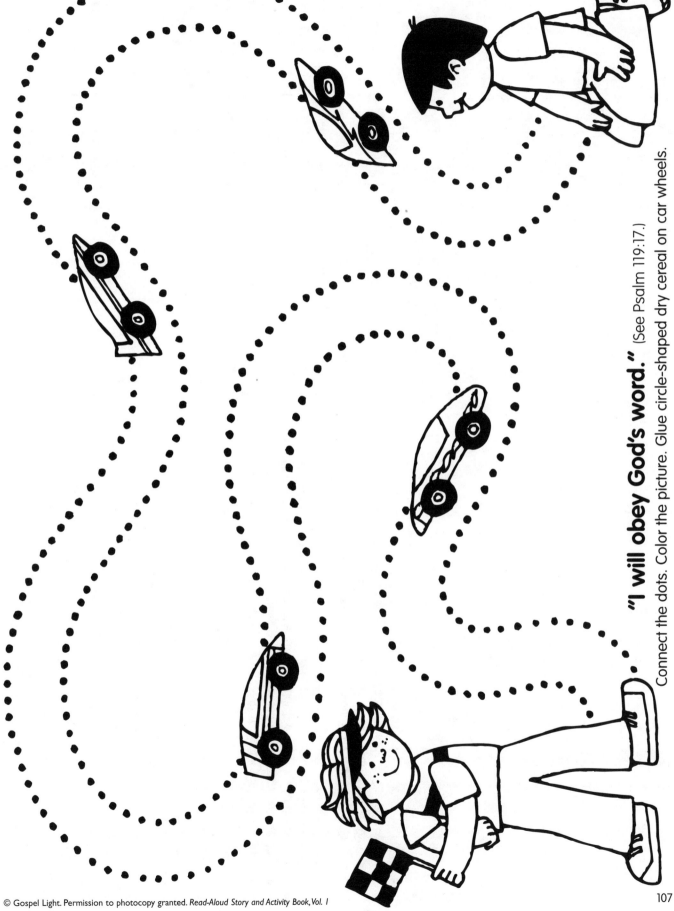

"I will obey God's word." (See Psalm 119:17.)

Connect the dots. Color the picture. Glue circle-shaped dry cereal on car wheels.

Read-Aloud Story and Activity

1. Make a copy of Story Picture 51 for yourself and each child. Gather materials; color and complete your copy.

2. **Listen to find out where Daniel took a car.** Read story and show completed Story Picture 51.

3. Distribute materials. Use Let's Talk About the Story ideas as children complete pictures.

The Little Red Car

Zoom, zoom, zoom went the cars on Kyle's racetrack. "Here comes the little red car—fast!" Daniel said as he gave the little red car a push, Zoom, zoom, zoom. Around the track it went.

Daniel and Kyle had a good time all afternoon playing at Kyle's house. They played with his racecars. Now it was time for Daniel to go home. Daniel looked at the little red car. He wished he had one like it! Kyle wasn't looking. He was putting away the racetrack. Daniel slipped the little red car into his pocket.

On the way home Daniel and his dad talked about going to the zoo on Saturday. And Daniel forgot he had the little red car in his pocket.

After dinner, Daniel went into his room. He remembered the little red car. He took it out of his pocket. He could hear his mom talking on the phone. She was saying, "I'll ask Daniel if he has seen Kyle's little red car." When she hung up the phone, she came into Daniel's room. Daniel hid the little red car behind his back.

"Daniel, that was Kyle's mother calling," Mom said. "Kyle can't find his little red car. Have you seen it?"

Daniel wished he had not taken Kyle's little red car! He remembered that God's Word said not to take things that were not his. He knew Kyle knew that from Sunday School, too. He brought the car out from behind his back.

"Is this Kyle's car?" Mom wanted to know.

"Yes," Daniel said softly.

"What should you do with it?" Mom asked.

"Give it back to Kyle," Daniel answered.

"Let's go to Kyle's house right now," Mom said, "so you can return his car. And if you are really sorry, you'll need to tell Kyle."

Daniel was quiet as he and Mom rode to Kyle's house. As they drove, Daniel told God he was sorry. Now he felt better. He gave the little red car back to Kyle and told Kyle he was sorry.

Kyle said, "It's OK. God's Word says I should forgive you. So I do!"

Let's Talk About the Story

What were Daniel and Kyle playing? What did Daniel take home with him? Who did the car belong to? How did Mom know about the little red car? How did Daniel feel about taking it? What did he do with the little red car? What did Daniel say in his prayer? Then how did he feel?

One way to show God's love to others is by helping them remember what God's Word says. Our Bible says, "I will obey God's word." Let's say this Bible verse together. Repeat Bible verse with children. **Let's pray. We'll ask God to help us love people and obey His Word.** Pray briefly.

"With love, help each other."

(See Galatians 5:13.)
How many fish are in the lake?
Connect the dots. Color the picture.

How many fish?

Read-Aloud Story and Activity

1. Make a copy of Story Picture 52 for yourself and each child. Gather materials; color and complete your copy.

2. **Listen for ways this boy helped.** Read story and show completed Story Picture 52.

3. Distribute materials. Use Let's Talk About the Story ideas as children complete pictures.

The Fishing Trip

One day Daddy said, "Uncle Ben and I are going fishing Friday."

"May I go, Daddy?" Connor asked. "Please?"

"Are you sure you really want to go? You know we'll be staying overnight and you'll have to sleep in the station wagon," Daddy answered.

"That's all right," Connor said. "Please let me go. You said I'm a good helper on trips."

"Yes, you are," Daddy said. "OK, Connor, you may go." Connor jumped up and down. He could hardly wait.

At last Friday came. It took a long time to get ready, but finally Uncle Ben, Connor and Daddy were in the station wagon. It was fun riding bumpety, bumpety through the woods to the big blue lake! Connor helped his dad set up camp. Connor helped gather firewood. Crackle, crackle went the fire. How good their dinner smelled—and it tasted even better!

The next day was the best day Connor ever had. Daddy showed him how to thread worms on his fish hook. Connor caught the very first fish! And that day he caught, not just one fish, but THREE!

Early the next morning Daddy said, "We'd better start home now."

Bumpety, bumpety went the station wagon back over the rough road to the highway. Then BANG went the tire. Sssss, sssss, sssss went the air, right out of the tire. Daddy stopped the car and they all got out.

"A flat tire!" Daddy said. "We'll have to fix it."

"I know how to help," Connor said.

"Let's get busy," said Uncle Ben. "First, Connor, find two big rocks to put under the wheels, so they won't roll."

Connor looked until he found two rocks just the right size. Then Daddy and Uncle Ben jacked the car up off the ground. As Daddy unscrewed the nuts from the wheel, Connor carefully dropped each one in the hubcap—plunk, plunk, plunk. Then Uncle Ben took off the flat tire and put on the spare tire.

"Connor, we need to put the nuts back on the bolts," Daddy said. Connor picked up each nut from the hubcap. He helped Daddy screw the nuts on. Then Daddy took a wrench and tightened each one.

"Now, Connor, you may push this little handle on the jack right here," Uncle Ben said. Connor did just what Uncle Ben told him. The wheel came very slowly down to the ground. Soon they were on their way home again. "Connor was a very good helper on this trip," said Uncle Ben.

"He sure was," said Daddy. "I can't wait to take him fishing again!

Let's Talk About the Story

Where did Connor go with Daddy and Uncle Ben? Where did Connor have to sleep? What did Connor learn to do? How many fish did Connor catch? What happened on the way home? How did Connor help?

It's good to be a helper. It shows our love for God. Our Bible says, **"With love, help each other." Let's say this Bible verse together.** Repeat Bible verse with children. **We can thank God for times we can help.** Pray briefly.

Bible Verse Index

Topical Index